Elections in Cyberspace:
Toward a New Era in American Politics

A Report of
The Aspen Institute
Communications and Society Program
and
The American Bar Association
Standing Committee on Election Law

Anthony Corrado
and
Charles M. Firestone
Editors

American Bar Association

Standing Committee on
Election Law
Pauline A. Schneider
Chair

The
Aspen
Institute

Communications and Society
Program
Charles M. Firestone
Director

For additional copies of this report, please contact:

The Aspen Institute
Publications Office
109 Houghton Lab Lane
P.O. Box 222
Queenstown, MD 21658
Phone: (410) 820-5326
Fax: (410) 827-9174
E-mail: publications@aspeninst.org

For all other inquiries, please contact:

The Aspen Institute
Communications and Society Program
Suite 1070
1333 New Hampshire Avenue, NW
Washington, DC 20036
Phone: (202) 736-5818
Fax: (202) 467-0790

Contents

Foreword

Communication and information have always been twin life forces of a healthy democracy. Candidates need the ability to communicate their messages to voters, and voters need the means to gather the information necessary to make intelligent decisions affecting their future. These are essential to the conduct of free and fair elections.

In recent years, however, there has been considerable voter disillusionment with the quality and quantity of useful information on which to make voting decisions and the mechanisms through which candidates and voters communicate about matters of civic concern. There is a general sense that candidates have gotten further away from the people, that their messages are truncated or filtered to the point of providing very little information of any real value to voters, and that the level of political discourse is below that which a leading democracy deserves. In general, there appears to be a distrust of the candidates and the media to give the voters what they need.

But there are powerful trends taking place in the ways in which people access information and communicate with one another that could revolutionize the political process. Among these trends, new communications and information technologies are making it cheaper to communicate with larger numbers of people, at a faster rate than ever before. These technologies make it possible to access information and to communicate with others at virtually any place and at any time that is convenient. In the process, they also are reversing the traditional flow of communication by empowering users to initiate dialogue and reducing the need for traditional intermediaries (such as journalists, editors, and other gatekeepers) to filter or alter political messages and information. Technologies have the ability to connect people and information in unprecedented ways.

But can new technologies really make a difference by providing hope for citizens to feel that they once again have an important voice in governance? Or will these new tools simply be used to exacerbate current practices that are turning voters away from the political process?

In an effort to explore some of the issues raised by these new technologies and to identify the concerns that should be addressed in their development, The Aspen Institute Communications and Society Program and the American Bar Association Standing Committee on Election Law, with the support of The John and Mary R. Markle Foundation, sponsored a conference of experts to discuss the implications of new forms of political communication. Specifically, the conference focused attention on the ways in which these new technologies may affect elections and campaigns. The goal was to identify the key issues that these changes are likely to engender for free and fair democratic elections and to define an agenda for further dialogue and action to ensure democratic, participatory, and fair elections in the future. The group included a diversity of perspectives, including leading experts in the areas of election law, campaigns, media, civic participation, and interactive communications. A complete list of conference participants follows the Appendix to this volume.

The Report

In this report, conference rapporteur and Colby College political science professor Anthony Corrado has deftly laid out the key issues involved in conducting political campaigns and elections in a digital environment, including the promises and dilemmas of the electronic republic. According to Corrado, who brings his considerable expertise in election law to bear on the comments and perceptions of conference participants, new communications and information technologies offer many opportunities for enhancing the quality of political communication in the United States and increasing citizen involvement in the political process. These include greater access to candidates and the electoral process;

better information on candidates, ballot issues, and government services; cheaper and faster candidate access to voters; potentially greater ballot access for minor party candidates; electronic voting for referendums and political candidates; enhanced civic networking; and the creation of new communities of interest within the electorate to address issues of regional importance.

Many of these benefits have already been realized on a small scale through the adoption of electronic techniques for campaigning by candidates and limited experiments by state and local governments. Technologies can enable government to become more responsive to its constituents and more creative in addressing civic issues. Most importantly, Corrado suggests, "they have the potential to create a new model of politics and governance, a 'conversational democracy,' in which citizens and political leaders interact in new and exciting ways."

While the tenor of his report generally is optimistic about the increasing use of communications and information technologies, Corrado also addresses the potential dilemmas of a political process conducted at least in part in cyberspace. These include the increasing disparity between the "haves" and "have nots" in society, and the misuse and abuse of technology by unscrupulous candidates and citizens alike. Corrado questions the ability of current electronic systems to authenticate adequately the information that voters receive and to ensure the integrity of the process. And even though technology offers the promise of greater connectedness among individuals, the fast and ubiquitous spread of communication and information could lead to a greater distrust of authority than ever before. The anonymity and lack of accountability that mark the on-line environment could produce a mean-spirited and ineffective deliberative process that turns "communities of interest" into "special interests" and furthers the gridlock of recent years. Unauthorized campaign web pages, misleading information, and disguised sources can exacerbate the problems with the political process that many are troubled by today.

The questions posed by Corrado are these: Will these new forms of communication suggest the prospect of a revitalized democracy in which average citizens will have a powerful voice in political affairs? Or will they prove unable to provide the quality of information needed to promote a more informed citizenry, and only serve to undermine the individual's sense of community? Will they enhance the democratic spirit of America or further exacerbate the sense of isolation and alienation within the electorate?

We should point out that the project and the conference were aimed primarily at issues of the adequacy of election laws and regulations in the new digital era. It was beyond the scope of the group to suggest changes relating to news coverage of elections, including the new cyberspace venues such as *AllPolitics* and *PoliticsNow*. Cable News Network (CNN) reported, for example, that it received over 50 million "hits" on election night. Clearly, these sites are an increasingly important aspect of election coverage, and their impact should be subject to scrutiny.

Background Papers

The Aspen Institute commissioned several background papers for the conference which served as catalysts for the initial discussions. These are included in the Appendix to this volume. In the first paper, Sonia Jarvis offers an assessment of the impact that new communications and information technologies may have on the conduct of elections in the future. Her analysis is grounded in research that covers current demographic, political, and cultural trends, and her assessment offers optimism tempered by caution about the future vitality of the political process.

Jarvis' paper is followed by three different scenarios of elections in the future: Jeffrey Abramson's look at the election of 2000, Tracy Westen's snapshot of the election of 2004, and Nolan Bowie's look back from the election of 2008. Each scenario, in its own way, identifies the driving trends in campaign technology, voter behavior, and campaign strategies that have considerable implications for citizen participation in free, fair, and democratic elections. Each addresses the question, *What kind of a democracy do we want, and what part will technology play in helping to realize the vision of a strong and vibrant democracy for the future?* We offer these scenarios for the reader to consider the answer to this question.

Acknowledgments

We would like to thank the many people who have contributed to making this collaboration between The Aspen Institute and the American Bar Association such a successful experience for those involved. First, Steven Uhlfelder, past chair of the Standing Committee on Election Law, for his insights into the future of elections in cyberspace and efforts to get this project off the ground. We are grateful to the members of the Standing Committee on Election Law, its Advisory Commission, and conference participants representing other organizations for bringing their expertise to the development of the conference and the final report. Jeff Abramson, Nolan Bowie, Sonia Jarvis, and Tracy Westen all contributed outstanding papers for the conference, each in its own way a stimulant for our discussions and further thinking on the topics.

We are especially grateful to The Markle Foundation and to Edith Bjornson, Vice President and Senior Program Officer of the Foundation, for their generous support of this project. We were fortunate also to have three demonstrations of on-line political information during the conference, and thank those who took their time to educate us about the kind of political information and communication that is currently available in cyberspace: Catherine Clark of The Markle Foundation, for a demonstration of the Markle funded on-line game, *President 96;* Tracy Westen, for his demonstration of *The Democracy Network;* and Evans Witt of the ABC News/Washington Post/Newsweek on-line service, *ElectionLine* (now part of the *PoliticsNow* site).

Much of the success of this project is owed to project consultant and conference rapporteur Tony Corrado, whose work with both the Committee and the Communications and Society Program is deeply appreciated. Finally, we thank the current and former staff members of the Standing Committee on Election Law, Elizabeth Yang and Rich Mandelbaum, for their aid and guidance in the formation of the project, and of the Communications and Society Program, Amy Garmer for her substantive aid throughout the organization of the conference and editing of this volume, Gia Nolan, for her work in coordinating the conference and its aftermath, and W. Daniel Wright, manager of The Aspen Institute Publications Office, for his production work on this report.

CHARLES M. FIRESTONE
Director
The Aspen Institute
Communications and
Society Program

PAULINE A. SCHNEIDER
Chair
American Bar Association
Standing Committee on
Election Law

Elections in Cyberspace: Prospects and Problems

by Anthony Corrado

Emerging technologies are revolutionizing political communication. Cable television, direct broadcast satellites, electronic mail, and the Internet are creating powerful new links between citizens and politicians, offering voters access to vast amounts of information, a diversity of perspectives, and new forums for sharing ideas. Although these technologies are still in their formative stages, they are already redefining traditional forms of political activity and transforming the character of political dialogue. Indeed, digital technology may ultimately have a greater effect on the American political system than radio and television did earlier in this century. And what we are now witnessing is only the beginning.

With the development of fiber optics and digital compression, the boundaries between traditionally separate electronic media, such as television, telephony, and computer networks, are breaking down. The result will be an interactive, multimedia environment in which average citizens will have on-demand access to video, audio, text, or data transmissions with the click of a hand-held remote control or portable computer keyboard. In this environment, citizens will communicate with each other and their political leaders in ways that less than 25 years ago were considered more science fiction than science fact.

These new forms of communication suggest the prospect of a revitalized democracy in which average citizens will have a powerful voice in political affairs. Speaker of the House Newt Gingrich, for example, envisions the day when we will have a "virtual Congress" through which citizens can participate in House hearings, gain access to government documents on-line, and

1

contact their representatives by electronic means. Ross Perot believes that new technologies will lead to the creation of electronic town meetings in which citizens from different parts of the country will link together through computer networks and television signals not only to share their views with legislators, but even to initiate and vote on proposed legislation. Still others look forward to a time when voters will be able to cast their ballot or vote on issue referendums through computer networks or over the telephone, thereby eliminating the physical and procedural barriers that have limited civic participation in the past.

While most observers agree that the digital revolution will dramatically transform American politics, there is wide disagreement about the effects of these changes. Many political experts believe that the primary effect will be to promote the development of a more democratic system of government. In this view, technology will close the gap between citizens and their government, making it easier for voters to communicate with political leaders and easier for these leaders to reflect the preferences of their constituents. Individuals will play a more meaningful role in political life, in part because they will not have to rely on pre-digested broadcast media or broad-based political party organizations to represent their views. Interactive media will increasingly replace more passive forms of political communication, which in turn will encourage the development of a more informed and active citizenry. Individual voters will have the capacity to identify issues of common interest and organize around them. They will be better able to hold officials accountable for their actions or to act when government fails to respond to their needs. The result will be a political system that promotes civic participation, responds to majority concerns, and provides individuals with a meaningful voice in the governing process.

Other practitioners are not so optimistic. While they agree that new technologies will expand public access to information, they are concerned that this information will only benefit a relatively small portion of the electorate. Many voters will not take advantage of the opportunities to learn more about candidates and government, and millions may not have access due to a lack of computer literacy skills or the unavailability of the necessary equipment.

Instead of promoting a more informed electorate and widespread participation, these experts believe that new technologies will primarily serve to enhance the strength of organized groups and further fragment the electorate. In addition, the immediate public feedback available to politicians will essentially constitute daily opinion polls, which may so closely tie legislators to constituent concerns that legislative compromise and consensus may be even more difficult to achieve than in the highly partisan, "gridlocked" governments of recent years.

Advocates believe that new technologies will stimulate greater civic participation and eventually make possible some form of electronic democracy. Yet, if the promise of an electronic democracy is achieved, the result may be a political system characterized by many of the problems first identified by the nation's founders over 200 years ago. The U.S. government is based on a system of checks and balances designed to filter public opinion and thwart majority impulses that might threaten the rights of minorities. An electronic democracy could undermine the delicate balance built into the present system by facilitating the type of direct majority rule that could affect minorities or lead to the adoption of policies that may not serve the nation's long-term interests. Thus, new technologies will require a rethinking of checks and balances, as well as other regulations that have been adopted to protect the fairness and integrity of the political system. Without such a reassessment, valuable procedural safeguards may be lost and any potential salutary effects of interactive methods of communication may not be achieved.

THE EMERGENCE OF CAMPAIGNS
IN CYBERSPACE

Electronic and digital forms of communication are rapidly emerging as important political tools, as an increasing number of citizens are gaining access to new information technologies. Over 20 million Americans already have access to the Internet, a world-wide computer network, through their home, school, or business, and this number is expected to grow dramatically over the next ten years. Over 30 percent of the households in the United States now own a personal computer, a percentage that is projected to rise to at least 67 percent by the year 2010.[1] Over 10 million households subscribe to an on-line service, a number which is expected to more than triple to 35.2 million by the year 2000.[2]

Many of those who will not have computers in their home by the turn of the century will be able to access information networks either from their business or in some other way. For example, in the next five years most public school systems should be on-line. More than half of the nation's public schools are already connected to the Internet, including nine percent of all classrooms, three times the percentage of just two years ago. To spur this growth, the federal government has launched an initiative to have every public school wired to the network by 2000, and many local governments and private businesses are working with federal agencies to make this goal a reality. Public libraries and hospitals are also expanding their efforts to make computer information technology more readily available to the public.

The expansion of on-line services and the great potential of the Internet as a means of communicating with voters has convinced many candidates, party organizations, and political groups to experiment with this technology. While World Wide Web sites, electronic bulletin boards, and other forms of interactive communication were regarded as novelties in the 1994 election cycle, they have gained much broader use in the 1996 campaigns. Indeed, they have reached a point where they have become a part of the presidential campaign, as well as many federal and state-wide contests. Even candidates for local office are beginning to explore ways of using digital communications to provide voters with information about their campaigns. These rudimentary efforts offer a glimpse of what political campaigning may be like in the near future.

During the 1996 presidential primary campaign, every one of the major Republican candidates established a web site on the Internet to distribute information and receive feedback from voters. One of the most developed sites is the one maintained by the Bob Dole for President campaign, which offers many of the features that are rapidly becoming common components of campaign web sites. Visitors to the Dole home page can view a pictorial biography of Senator Dole, access reports on the campaign's state-by-state progress, and make use of a "Dole Library" from which they can simply view or download press releases, position papers, and audio or video clips from a digital archive. They can also subscribe to an electronic mail newsletter, pledge a contribution on-line, or volunteer to host an event in their homes, place a sign on their front lawn, or help get out the vote on election day. While the overall effect of such a site is impossible to assess, the Dole campaign reported that its home page received more than 3 million hits during its first six months of operation, with over 10,000 people joining the electronic mail list and 1,700 registering to serve as volunteers.[3]

The Buchanan for President campaign was even more aggressive in using the Internet to recruit volunteers and inform voters. Unlike the Dole site, the Buchanan home page was created and maintained by volunteers and supporters, and therefore serves as a better reflection of the kinds of public outreach and grass roots activity that are possible with current digital technology. The site offered information on how to join various state "Buchanan Brigades," provided membership forms, presented bulletin boards for networking with other supporters, and contained an electronic mail box for delivering messages to the campaign. In addition, the site instructed supporters on how to recruit other voters, and included messages that urged them to pursue alternative means of spreading the Buchanan message, such as starting electronic news groups devoted to Buchanan and uploading information about him onto commercial on-line services such as America Online and CompuServe.

President Bill Clinton's reelection campaign did not set up a web site during the primaries. But voters interested in learning more about the President could access the White House home page, which routinely provides a substantial amount of information about the President and his administration. This site includes transcripts of speeches, daily press releases, copies of government agency reports, and summaries of administration accomplishments, as well as pictures of the First Family and information from the Vice President's Office. The White House also established an electronic mail service and bulletin boards that citizens can use to send messages to the President or Vice President. They have also explored more advanced capabilities of the new technology by holding cyberspace press conferences in which journalists from around the country could ask questions of administration officials on-line, as well as cyberspace conferences linking administration officials and citizens from around the country in electronic forums.

The contest for the White House is not the only race being run at least in part on the information highway. Many members of Congress and congressional candidates have home pages on the Internet, as do hundreds of other political leaders. By the end of January 1996, more than 70 Senators and close to 200 Members of Congress had established electronic mail systems or web sites to facilitate communications with constituents. Party organizations are also taking advantage of this new resource. The Democratic and Republican National Committees have established sites that include many of the features found on individual candidate home pages, including extensive information archives that make press releases, policy papers, and party platform statements available to a wide audience.

The two major parties are not alone in cyberspace. Many minor parties, such as Ross Perot's Reform Party, the Libertarian Party, the Natural Law Party, and the Green Party, are also using the web to spread their messages. So too are interest groups and lobbying organizations, including the National Rifle Association, National Organization of Women, Sierra Club, and Christian Coalition, all of which are using the Internet to recruit support, distribute information, maintain contact with members, track legislation, and organize efforts to influence legislators.

In the future, these uses of digital technology will be supplemented by even more impressive communication capabilities. For example, the Center for Governmental Studies, a non-profit organization devoted to the improvement of media and governing processes, has begun to develop and implement an interactive video, textual, and audio political information system designed for use on both the World Wide Web and broadband cable and telephone networks. Called *The Democracy Network*, it is now being implemented as part of Time Warner's Full Service Network interactive television experiment in Orlando, Florida, and was available to provide subscribers with information related to the 1996 presidential election, as well as some state and local elections. This system would allow voters, through their computers or television sets, to select and review video, audio, and textual materials from local, state, and federal government officials and political candidates; to view independent television, radio, and newspaper materials on candidates, policy issues, or government programs; and to communicate with elected officials, candidates, and other citizens in electronic town halls. *The Democracy Network*—or similar programs—could thus provide voters with a comprehensive, wholly interactive political information service. Voters would be able to review candidate statements, position papers, organizational endorsements, or newspaper articles on particular issues; watch video presentations of campaign speeches or a candidate's statements on the key issues in a race; review news stories and newspaper editorials in video or textual formats; and even ask questions of candidates through electronic means. The system would also give users access to electronic bulletin boards or chat rooms where particular issues or candidates can be discussed.

While the use of the Internet and other interactive technologies is spreading rapidly, it is unlikely that they will have a major effect on political campaigning in the next few years. The portion of the electorate with access to these technologies is still relatively small, and only a minor percentage of users rely on these methods for political information. But many experts anticipate that they will constitute an important aspect of electoral politics as soon as the year 2000. Although they will not have replaced television and radio as the major sources of voter information by that time, they will be an important source of information for a significant share of the electorate and a primary component of an increasing number of campaigns.

Candidates and political groups will continue to adopt and place greater emphasis on digital, interactive means of communication for a number of reasons. Because some candidates are already employing these methods, others are following their lead either due to fear of being placed at some strategic disadvantage or because they recognize the potential of these technologies for reaching out to select groups of voters. These incentives will be even more compelling as more voters gain access to these methods. Technological developments will spur this growth by expanding availability and increasing the ways in which voters can access interactive media, while at the same time reducing equipment costs. As one conference participant noted, by 2010 gaining access to digital information may be as easy as picking up a telephone or selecting a channel on a television set.

REVIVING DEMOCRATIC POLITICS

The primary reason why interactive communications will likely come to the fore in electoral and governmental politics is that candidates and voters alike are beginning to recognize and experience their advantages over television, radio, surface mail and other current methods of political outreach. These advantages are already apparent in the limited uses now being explored, and they should increase dramatically as the technology develops.

Reconnecting the Citizenry

Opinion poll after opinion poll has demonstrated that large majorities of Americans feel alienated and distant from the political process. Gone are the days when most voters personally knew an individual seeking office or had a chance to meet a candidate face-to-face. Presidential campaigns have largely become a series of tarmac photo opportunities and 30-second television ads. Even in statewide races, few voters get a chance to ask a candidate a question or discuss a particular concern.

Emerging technologies offer a means of reestablishing the connection between voters and candidates. While not as intimate as meetings in person, they allow a type of individual contact and interaction that is not possible through current campaign communications. Voters can ask specific questions of candidates and acquire information on topics of particular interest to them. Through electronic mail and town meetings they can engage in dialogues with candidates or elected officials. Furthermore, since citizens with access to the Internet will have a capacity to share their views with, potentially, millions of other voters, they can also participate in broader public dialogues about politics and elections.

Improving Voter Information

Promoting the development of an informed electorate is one of the basic objectives of a democratic political process. But most observers argue that this goal is not being fulfilled by the current system. Voters now receive the bulk of their political information from news reports or candidate-sponsored television and radio advertising, which are widely criticized as not conducive to the creation of a more enlightened public. Instead of providing voters with detailed information on policy issues and the candidates' respective positions on major public concerns, news reports increasingly tend to reduce candidate speeches or statements to brief "sound bites," emphasize the tactical and strategic aspects of political campaigns, and devote relatively little attention to the substance of policy debates. The brief, 30-second format of most campaign ads offers even less substantive information to voters. And, according to many experts, the rise of negative advertising has further diminished the quality of political discourse in this nation, while at the same time it has increased public disaffection with politics and reduced the level of political participation.

The expansion of digital communications will dramatically change the quality of the information readily available to voters. With the rise of the Internet and continuing expansion of cable television alternatives, citizens will have access to a wide range of information from a variety of sources. In fact, the materials prepared by candidates, party organizations, and other partisan groups will be but the tip of the information iceberg in the dynamic, multimedia environment of the future. These materials will be supplemented by information prepared by a wide spectrum of political groups, citizens' associations, and news organizations. This will provide voters with greater access to contrasting views and enhance their ability to compare candidates' views on particular issues. As a result, the public will be able to achieve more well-rounded views of those seeking political office.

Examples of the type of higher quality information that will be available to voters already can be seen on the World Wide Web. Project Vote Smart, a nonprofit organization, has established a web site that offers users a wide array of factual information on federal and statewide elected officials and candidates from all fifty states. The site includes biographical backgrounds, voting records, interest group ratings, and campaign finance data, as well as links to home pages of candidates, all branches of the federal government, and state government election sites. A number of news organizations have joined forces, among them, CNN and *Time Magazine,* and the *Washington Post* and ABC News, to develop multimedia sites devoted to political coverage that include video and audio clips, transcripts of news broadcasts, and background information on stories in the news, as well as links to candidate home pages and other political information sites. Over time, such sites will enable voters to gain additional information on major news stories, contrast the policy views of different candidates, compare candidates' campaign pledges to their voting records in office, and track a candidate's financial support and policy positions from election to election.

Moreover, as a number of conference participants noted, much of the information that will be distributed through the Internet or other interactive means will be "unmediated"; that is, it will not go through the editorial process that currently shapes much news reporting or be oriented towards particular views or interests. Instead, voters will be able to decide for themselves what information they consider to be most important. The advent of politics in cyberspace and digital technology will thus create a revitalized arena of free political speech that will help voters develop more informed views.

Increasing Candidate Access to the Political Process

One of the primary reasons why the information environment is likely to change in the future is the reduced cost of political communications. Unlike television and radio advertising, distributing information via the World Wide Web is relatively inexpensive. Anyone with the proper software can place a message on an electronic bulletin board or newsgroup, or send thousands of electronic mail messages without the printing and postage costs of surface mail. Individuals can also post messages on web sites that solicit visitor responses or create web sites of their own. In addition, the cost to a campaign of creating and maintaining a web site is much less than the cost of producing and airing even a single television ad, and dramatically less than the cost of even a modest television advertising campaign.[4]

Because of their low cost, new technologies will open the electoral process to groups and candidates who have traditionally been priced out of the mass political market. As one conference participant noted, digital communications could make financial resources less important in electoral politics since candidates will have access to mass audiences without having to conduct expensive advertising campaigns or spend tens of thousands of dollars on direct mail. While this advantage is unlikely to be achieved in the near term due to the likelihood of continued reliance on television advertising and other traditional forms of communication, it is clearly the case that emerging technologies will benefit candidates who lack significant financial resources or broad-based public support.

The Internet is already becoming a principal means of communication for those who have traditionally been unable to generate or purchase significant media attention. Among others, the Libertarian Party, Natural Law Party, and Green Party are using the Internet to spread their messages, maintain contact with members, and recruit new supporters. These parties, which traditionally have not had the resources to engage in mass public advertising, can now present their candidates and their views to an audience that could potentially reach tens of millions of voters. They thus hope to gain in the future the exposure they lacked in past elections due to their inability to generate significant media attention or attract a substantial share of the vote.

The potential effectiveness of this approach is suggested by the experience of United We Stand America, the citizens' group formed by Ross Perot after the 1992 election, and, more recently, the Reform Party. Although atypical of other minor parties in many regards, these organizations stand as prime examples of the type of intraparty activity that can be achieved through the World Wide Web. In the 1996 election cycle, the Reform Party has used this vehicle for communicating with state coordinators and supporters, recruiting and coordinating the activities of volunteers, responding to requests for information, distributing its statement of principles and press releases, informing users of upcoming Perot events and media appearances, and providing updates on ballot access efforts and party convention planning. The site has also spurred party members to create web sites of their own, which gather and distribute articles about Perot and the Reform Party, and spread the word about the new party. The party even plans to use the Internet as a means of allowing its members to participate in party decision-making; for example, as part of the selection process for the party's 1996 presidential nominee, members could inform the national headquarters of their candidate preference by casting votes via the Internet.

In the future, digital communications may not just facilitate the growth of current political organizations, it could also stimulate the creation of new parties and political institutions. The most basic feature of this technology is that it will allow individuals more easily to find others who share their interests or views and communicate with them, which in turn will lead to the development of new forms of "community," new political groups, and, undoubtedly, new political organizations. Indeed, as many conference participants noted, in the future the political system may no longer be dominated by the Democratic and Republican parties. Instead, a variety of political communities and party interests could emerge, many of which would transcend geographic or political boundaries. These may include a Western Taxpayer's Rights Party, a Women's Party, a Citizens' Party, a Christian Coalition Party, or even a party devoted to the concerns of minority voters.

Expanding Voter Alternatives

Because a broader range of political groups and candidates will be able to reach large audiences, voters will have more candidates to choose from when they cast their ballots. This is likely to increase electoral competition and could help restore the public's faith in the American system of government. Currently, more than a third of the electorate no longer identifies with either of the two major parties, and a majority feels that the candidates who seek major office do not represent its interests or concerns. This lack of connectedness is often cited as one of the reasons why so many Americans feel alienated from politics and choose not to participate on Election Day. By expanding the choices available to the electorate, new technologies will make it more likely that groups of voters will find candidates whom they feel are more representative of their views. Interactive communications may even encourage candidates to orient their campaigns towards the representation of particular blocs of voters or to stake out clear policy positions in hopes of building new electoral coalitions. These outcomes may very well rekindle public interest in election campaigns, and make elections more competitive, which would encourage larger numbers of citizens to turn out and vote.

Increasing Civic Participation

The digital revolution could also promote civic involvement simply by making it easier to participate. Rather than relying solely on elected officials, party organizations, or organized interest groups to represent their views, citizens can present their own views through electronic messages that will provide candidates and legislators with immediate feedback. They can also take part in electronic town halls, where they can discuss political issues with citizens and government officials from their local community, region, and state, or from throughout the nation. In addition, the technology can also be used to revitalize civic life by encouraging broad participation in a variety of political activities.

FUNDRAISING

One form of political participation that could easily be encouraged by electronic communications is the act of making a financial contribution to a candidate or political organization. Candidates and groups could solicit hundreds of thousands of potential donors through their web sites or via electronic mail without having to incur the expense of telephone campaigns or direct mail solicitations. Such methods of solicitation would dramatically reduce the cost of campaign fundraising and enhance the possibility of financing a viable political campaign through thousands of small contributions.

The potential efficacy of electronic fundraising efforts can be illustrated by the 1992 presidential campaign of former California governor Jerry Brown. Brown's organization raised millions of dollars in contributions of $100 or less through creative use of a 24-hour-a-day 800 telephone number, direct mail, and televised info-mercials. Another example is the political action committee (PAC) Newtwatch, which was established to distribute information about Speaker of the House Newt Gingrich over the World Wide Web. This committee, which is the first of its kind to be established in cyberspace and conduct financial activities in cyberspace, solicits contributions on-line, with deposits made through an independent company directly into the PAC's account via credit card transactions. In response to the creation of this unique PAC and in an effort to meet the expected needs of the future, the Federal Election Commission in 1995 developed guidelines for soliciting contributions over the Internet. It is only a matter of time before candidates, parties, and a wide range of political groups begin to explore the potential of fundraising over the Internet.

Whether on-line transactions will develop into an effective means of raising political funds remains to be seen, but if it does prove to be effective, it is certain that many candidates and political committees will begin to adopt this approach. Given the efforts now underway to facilitate secure financial transactions over the Internet and promote the use of "electronic money," it is likely that electronic fundraising will become a vital tool in political campaigns. New technologies may thus stimulate the type of broad financial participation and small-donor based fundraising that was envisioned by the campaign finance laws of the 1970s.

ELECTRONIC VOTING

As digital technology continues to develop, there is no reason why citizens will not be able to register to vote electronically or even be registered automatically based on driver's license information or other official government records. We are already moving in this direction, as evidenced by the adoption of the motor voter law and the movement towards same-day voter registration, or the recent experiments in Oregon and a number of local communities with mail balloting. But even these pathbreaking reforms, which are designed to remove registration as an obstacle to voting and encourage higher participation, seem cumbersome when compared to the changes on the horizon.

States are already beginning to experiment with ways to use new technologies to increase voter registration. Oregon and California, for example, have placed voter registration information and voter guides on the World Wide Web. In 1995, South Carolina became the first state to offer computer-assisted voter registration. Under its system, prospective voters can obtain voter registration forms via the Internet, print them out on their personal computers, sign them and mail them to election administrators. Voter registration administrators will not be able to forgo the interim step of a paper form until the technology for a secure "electronic signature" is perfected. But this process is already well underway. The Internal Revenue Service and many private companies are now testing various signature-verification schemes that would allow wholly electronic registration in the future.[5]

Once a secure system for verifying signatures and protecting the integrity of the ballot is developed, voting by electronic means will also be possible. Voters will be able to download a ballot from an approved government web site (probably maintained by the secretary of state's office or local county registrar) and cast their votes over the Internet, or be able to call a toll-free voter number and, after providing some type of specialized voter identification number, punch in their votes via the telephone. Such processes will essentially eliminate the physical barriers to voting, the time needed to cast a ballot, or any other inconveniences, such as the need to cast a vote on a specific day during a limited time period.

This should have the effect of increasing voter turnout substantially. Electronic voting will also dramatically reduce the cost of administering elections, with some estimates predicting that it may reduce per-vote cost of an election by as much as 75 percent.[6]

ELECTRONIC INITIATIVES AND REFERENDUMS

Perhaps most importantly, a wired republic will also allow citizens to take a more active and substantive role in their own governance. In particular, they will have the capacity to take legislative decision-making into their own hands by initiating proposals and considering public referendums electronically. Groups or individuals could meet on-line to discuss issues and develop initiatives or proposals. These proposals could then be circulated through an on-line petition process in which registered voters could either sign a petition and pass it on to others via electronic means, or add their signatures to a list maintained at established web sites. Any petition that received enough signatures to meet a preestablished threshold could then be eligible for submission to the appropriate legislative or executive agency for further consideration. Or it could qualify for a direct popular vote, with the support of a certain percentage of the voting age public needed to pass it into law.

An electronic initiative and referendum process of this sort certainly would require a major rethinking of referendum procedures and the applicability of current state and local petition requirements. It might even lead to the adoption of a national referendum process. According to one recent survey, Americans favor the creation of a national referendum process by the wide margin of 76 percent to 19 percent.[7] Future technology will make nationwide referendums possible. But whether lawmakers will approve such a radical change in government decision-making remains to be seen.

Advocates argue that an electronic referendum process should be established since it could play a vital role in making the American political system more responsive to public concerns.

Citizens would be better able to demonstrate their support for particular policy proposals, which might convince legislators to take action to meet the public's demands. Or, if legislators or government agencies fail to reach agreement on proposed legislation or refuse to enact a particular bill, citizens could take action on their own, placing the proposal before the electorate for a vote.

Electronic voting and on-line referendums might also make government more responsive by allowing political issues to be addressed on more representative bases. For example, it might allow citizens and elected officials to address issues outside of the constraints of geographical or political boundaries. Local issues affecting only a few sections of a large urban area could be addressed by the citizens and representatives of the affected areas in a specially demarcated electronic forum. Regional issues could be addressed on a regional basis, instead of on the basis of several separate local or urban divisions that now characterize much policy-making. Technological change may thus bring about greater flexibility in governing and more creative ways of addressing civic issues.

New technologies can thus help to restore the democratic culture of our politics by reviving the role of the people in elections and governance. They can provide the citizenry with the information and choices needed to yield the kind of meaningful and competitive elections that are the lifeblood of a representative electoral process. Most importantly, they have the potential to create a new model of politics and governance, a "conversational democracy," in which citizens and political leaders interact in new and exciting ways. In this model, individual citizens will be able to gather information easily from a variety of sources, and communicate directly with other citizens locally or throughout the nation. The Internet can thus facilitate the development of countless streams of political dialogue and debate that will help promote civic awareness and participation. Citizens will also be able to interact more directly with candidates, party organizations, and other political groups than is the case under the current system of broadcast communications, while political leaders can provide a regular flow of information to voters. In short, in this system, public life will be carried out through the type of dialogue and interaction that our nation's founders envisioned as the essence of democratic governance.

EMERGING AND FUTURE POLICY CONCERNS

While emerging technologies offer new hope for improving the political system, they also raise many fundamental concerns. Is a new regulatory structure needed to govern the types of political activity that are possible in cyberspace? Will the new communications revolution ensure equitable access to political information? Will it provide the quality of information needed to promote a more informed citizenry? Will it undermine an individual's sense of physical community and thereby exacerbate the sense of isolation and alienation within the electorate?

In attempting to answer these questions, the conference participants identified a number of issues that should serve as the focal points of future decision-making regarding the development of interactive political communications.

Ensuring Fair and Equitable Access

As an increasing amount of political activity and communication begins to take place in cyberspace, fair and equitable access to new technologies will become an increasingly important concern. A number of conference participants observed that we face the risk of a divided electorate, split between those who have access to technology and those who do not, or a split between those who are computer literate and those who are not. If such a division does transpire, certain segments of the electorate may be disadvantaged because they will not have ready access to the same information and will not be able to participate politically in the same way as others. Such disparities in the opportunity to participate, as well as in actual participation itself, would raise serious questions about the fairness and equity of the electoral process.

Many observers believe that any inequities in the level of voter information access currently being projected will be solved in due course by market mechanisms and the sorts of public/private initiatives that are already underway. As with first radio and then television, there will be a transitional period in which a minority of voters will enjoy significantly greater access than others. But soon the technology will become commonplace and increasingly

affordable, making it unlikely that there will be significant disparities among different groups of voters or geographical areas.
Furthermore, even if voters do not have access in their own homes,
public availability through schools, libraries, kiosks, town offices,
and other venues will be extensive enough to ensure an appropriate level of access for all citizens who seek it.

Other conference members, however, noted that fair and
equitable access is by no means guaranteed and that one of the
imperatives in developing these new technologies as vehicles for
political communication should be to guarantee such access. As
one participant observed, digital telecommunications differ from
radio and television in that there is currently no common carrier
broadcasting network involved; the wire services involved in cable
and digital communications are generally private companies. How
then do we guarantee right of access? How do we ensure service
in areas that would not be profitable to corporate providers? While
it may be the case that some access could be obtained through
libraries or school systems, these local institutions are already
facing severe resource problems and it is unlikely that they will
have the funds needed to guarantee even a minimal level of
widespread public access any time in the near future. In addition,
the rise of private on-line services and the growing privatization or
commoditization of information may serve to reduce the amount
of free information that is available to the public, in effect denying
it to those who cannot pay for it.

Even if individuals can get the hardware needed to access
information networks, some participants were concerned that
many citizens would not be able to use it. Particular note was made
of the significant percentage of Americans, at least 20 percent, who
are illiterate and thus incapable of using print-based systems and
formats because of their inability to read. An even larger share of
the electorate is considered functionally illiterate. This raises the
question of whether a significant minority of voters will be unable
to learn the basic skills needed to use new information technologies, never mind gain a level of proficiency that will allow them to
take advantage of the benefits these technologies have to offer.

These issues may be partially resolved in the future by non-
print-based command and control systems, and by the availability

of video, audio, and other, less text-based methods of information distribution. Indeed, emerging technologies may actually help to enrich the quality of political participation for many of these individuals by providing a means by which they can access information without having to rely on print-based systems. Whatever the case, the issue of equitable access should be a primary consideration in the future development of new political technologies, since a failure to address this concern will undermine the fairness of the political process and significantly reduce the potential of these technologies to promote a more widely informed and active electorate.

Ensuring the Integrity and Quality of Information

Providing access is only the first step in realizing the potential of new technologies to create a more informed electorate. The availability of accurate and meaningful information must also be guaranteed. This is a goal that is not easily achieved, especially in an era of interactive communications.

One of the great advantages of the Internet and electronic mail is that any individual has a capacity to communicate with large groups, even millions, of other citizens. This is also one of the Internet's great weaknesses. The World Wide Web is essentially an anarchic network of computers that allows for a virtually unlimited amount of information to be distributed and linked to documents and images from around the world. Because almost anyone is able to make information available to a worldwide audience through this means, a major concern is how to ensure the integrity and authenticity of the information that is publicly available.

This problem has already surfaced in the limited political use of the Internet now underway. Individuals have copied the home pages of some candidates and used them to create alternative sites designed to criticize or parody that candidate. For example, a seemingly authentic "Bob Dole for President" page appeared to be a site established by the Dole campaign. Instead, it was a copycat page that parodied the senator's bid for high office by linking him to Dole pineapples and other information on "fruits and vegetables" (http://www.dole96.org). Another site parodied the Buchanan for President page. In many instances, pages unauthorized by a campaign are created both for and against a candidate long before an official web site is established. These sites, which are unfiltered and unauthorized by any candidate or regulatory body, often contain unverified data, as well as information designed to discredit candidates and advance unsubstantiated rumors. Individuals could also compromise the integrity of information posted on the web by downloading an item, altering its content, and redistributing it as "authentic" information.

Consideration must therefore be given to the best ways to protect the integrity and ensure the authenticity of the information made available to the electorate through new interactive means. Many experts feel that this problem will be best addressed by the "free marketplace of ideas" that will exist on the World Wide Web. Unlike television, radio, or the types of print communications that are now used in campaigns, the Internet and other electronic communications offer the possibility of immediate side-by-side contrast and response. Just as citizens will be able to access the official messages of a candidate or campaign, they will also be able to see criticisms or responses issued by opposing candidates or other sources. Similarly, candidates will be able to post responses to unsolicited information or messages, providing their views on any issues raised and their rejoinders to any charges. Voters will thus be given the information they need to make their own decisions, based on a depth of information that is not now available.

Others fear that this "market place" scenario will be inadequate. They are concerned that voters will be more confused than enlightened by the competing claims and data that will be available. More important, they also argue that there are accountability issues that must be addressed. If the integrity of information placed on the web by candidates or political organizations can not be secured, can these individuals or organizations be held accountable for any and all information made accessible on their home page or through links to their web sites? Given the ability of individuals or groups to assume false identities or place information on the web anonymously, how does a voter or candidate know whom to hold accountable?

Conference participants observed that the first step in addressing these problems is to be found in the technical solution of improved security and protection programs designed to safeguard information from alteration or fraudulent use. Such systems will protect the authorized information posted by candidates and political groups from being tampered with, thereby making it possible to hold these agents accountable for any materials posted on their sites.

Another step may be to apply current regulatory principles to the new technologies. In the current regulatory regime established under the Federal Election Campaign Act, all federal candidates and political organizations, as well as groups or individuals who spend funds independently on advertisements or other materials that advocate the election or defeat of a federal candidate, must publicly disclose their spending to the Federal Election Commission and place a disclaimer on all advertising and print materials. The purpose of this law is to enable voters to identify sources of financial support and information, and thus be able to determine who is supporting or opposing a given candidate.

Some experts contend that a similar requirement or the same type of disclaimer should be applied to materials distributed over the World Wide Web, so that the public is aware of the source of the information. But one problem with this approach is that new technologies will encourage such broad participation that any mandate of this type is likely to be unenforceable. For the most part, those who engage in political advocacy in the current political system—candidates, party organizations, and political action committees—are politically sophisticated and cognizant of the regulations that govern their activities. New technologies will encourage thousands of other individuals or groups to share their political views and information with potentially large audiences. Few of these citizens, however, will have any experience with reporting requirements or other political regulations. Indeed, those who are experienced in web communications are used to an essentially unregulated, free speech environment, governed at best by ad hoc protocols and informal customs. Implementing a disclaimer or reporting requirement on such a dynamic process of political activity is therefore likely to be impossible.

Such a requirement might also have a "chilling effect" on political speech by discouraging many individuals from utilizing the new media for fear of transgressions, and thus diminish what most observers believe to be the greatest strength of this technology, its potential for wide participation. The reporting and disclaimer requirements of current law therefore need to be reviewed carefully both to determine their applicability to emerging technologies and to assess their potential consequences if applied to new methods of communicating.

Promoting Meaningful Civic Participation: The Need for Regulatory Reform

Although federal agencies may not be able to regulate the content of political information distributed via the World Wide Web, there are other steps they can take to improve the quality of voter information and promote political participation via electronic means. Most of these involve the revision of current statutes or regulations to ensure that these laws do not serve to discourage electronic forms of participation.

There are a number of aspects of campaign finance law that need to be reformed for the promise of an electronic republic to be achieved. First, the regulations governing the filing of campaign finance reports should be revised to provide for electronic filing of data. Currently most reporting by candidates or political committees is done on paper forms or hard copy computer printouts that are mailed or hand-delivered to the Federal Election Commission, in the case of federal candidates and elections, or the appropriate state or local disclosure agencies, in the case of nonfederal candidates. These reports are cumbersome to work with and difficult for most news reporters or individual citizens to access. In many states, citizens can only gain access to the information disclosed in these reports by paying for duplicated copies or visiting an official disclosure agency in person. As a result, financial disclosure, especially at the state level, has not proven to be as effective a vehicle for creating a more informed electorate as it could be.

By establishing appropriate procedures for electronic filing, disclosure agencies can make campaign finance data more readily accessible to the general public. The reports could then be filed in formats that can easily be distributed via electronic mail or over the Internet. The Federal Election Commission and state disclosure agencies should therefore encourage candidates to file reports electronically, not only by authorizing this process, but also by making filing software available to candidates and political committees free of charge and by offering training assistance.

Second, the Federal Election Commission should promulgate regulations governing electronic fundraising efforts. Although this is not a major source of campaign money at present, the expected growth in electronic banking and digital commerce make it a potentially lucrative source of political contributions in the future. The Commission should therefore review the guidelines it has developed to date and establish formal regulations to govern this type of financial activity. Furthermore, the agency should revise the current rules that do not allow credit card contributions to qualify for public matching funds in presidential elections. Allowing matching funds for these and other electronic contributions will give presidential candidates an incentive to use new technologies to solicit small donations, which may serve to broaden the level of citizen financial participation in future presidential races.

A third area of reform that needs to be considered concerns the regulations governing the role of corporations in the political process. The current law seeks to reduce the influence of corporate entities in political campaigns by preventing corporations from making either direct financial gifts or contributions of in-kind services to candidates for federal office. Yet this approach may prove incompatible with the efforts underway to promote political discourse through the expansion of new technologies. For example, millions of Americans will gain access to interactive communications through private on-line services or some other infrastructure that permits two-way communications. If one of these companies invites a candidate to provide materials for distribution through its service or creates a chat room in which citizens can hold an on-line conversation with a candidate, under current interpretations of the law the company may be guilty of providing an illegal in-kind contribution to that candidate. The law should be revised to accommodate new technologies and promote, rather than hinder, opportunities for interaction between candidates and voters.

Managing the Information Environment: New Forms of Community

One of the major drawbacks to interactive communications is that most of the methods involve time-consuming processes that require a relatively high level of motivation on the part of the user. It takes more time and commitment on the part of the individual to participate in an on-line political conversation, search for voting record information on the Internet, or correspond with an elected official by electronic means, than it does to watch the evening news broadcast, scan the newspaper headlines, or listen to a talk radio program. Will a significant number of citizens take advantage of the new technologies and spend the time needed to become better informed voters? Will they be motivated to use the information that is available to them?

This issue is likely to become more prominent as the political uses of new technologies increase and develop. As access to information continues to expand, individuals will increasingly face the problem of information overload. Their primary concern will be how to select, authenticate, interpret, and assess the information already available on demand, rather than that of how to gain access to information on government and politics. As a result, voters will have to find ways to manage information more efficiently.

To resolve this problem, voters will seek out shortcuts for obtaining the information they consider relevant and useful. This need might eventually be met through a technical solution, the use of "intelligent agents." Intelligent agents are autonomous, customizable software programs that can gather and synthesize information for their users. They can be programmed to search for information from particular sites on specific subjects, and form a digest for the individual user that can essentially serve as a daily, multimedia "newspaper." But this technology is still in its infancy, and it is unlikely that a significant portion of the electorate will have access to it any time in the near future.

The most likely response for most users will be to rely on specific web sites or sources for their information, just as they now rely on a certain evening news broadcasts or newspapers. But the sources are unlikely to be such traditional intermediaries as political parties, major network news associations, schools, or local civic organizations. Instead these links between citizens and government will be replaced by a vast array of formal and informal "neo-intermediaries," that can interact with each other freely without having to rely on traditional "gatekeepers" or institutions.

These "neo-intermediaries" will include many of the institutions that currently serve as mediators between the citizenry and elected officials or government institutions. This is evident from the activities of the last year in which many traditional press organizations have established World Wide Web sites and other interactive forms of communicating with voters. But it is also clear that a vast array of new actors or sources of political communication are rapidly emerging. These include networks and other interactive services maintained by online service providers, new corporate partnerships such as the one between Microsoft Corporation and NBC, and web sites established by partisan political organizations, private and public interest groups, and think tanks and foundations. In addition, less formal groups of citizens are gaining access to information and pursuing common interests by organizing themselves into "virtual communities" independent of the more structured forums provided by even the newest of neo-intermediaries.

While these new information vehicles and forms of community are often cast as one of the improvements that will accompany new technologies, they raise many questions that policymakers need to consider. What sorts of information will be accessible through these sites? Will they promote exposure to different perspectives and views? To what extent will they uphold notions of collective accountability and ethical standards, especially with respect to the distribution of unverified information or the acceptance of minority views? Will there be limitations or contractual rules placed upon participants?

These issues are especially important because they strike at the heart of the question of whether the digitally interactive politics of the future will actually improve the quality of American democracy. As a number of conference participants noted, emerging communications technologies may not lead to the broader, more informed public dialogue that many advocates envision. Instead, given so many possibilities and the prospect of information overload, most voters may continue to opt for information sources that essentially reflect their own views, and participate only in on-line forums that provide settings for meeting like-minded voters who will not criticize their thinking. If so, a major effect of interactive communications may prove to be greater fragmentation and disassociation of the electorate, rather than a more broadly informed, active public.

Preparing for an Electronic Democracy

Because there is no guarantee that new technologies will promote the type of widespread, more informed participation that advocates expect, policymakers should proceed with caution in their efforts to promote electronic democracy. While the technology offers exciting prospects for direct voter participation in on-line initiatives and referendums, conference participants were careful to note that there are a number of concerns that must be addressed before these processes are established as part of our system of governance.

First, existing procedures for popular initiatives and referendums include a wide range of traditional safeguards that are designed to ensure that these processes are not abused and that any initiative or referendum placed on the ballot enjoys support from a substantial share of the electorate. For example, petitioning procedures specify the number of valid signatures from registered voters needed to qualify an initiative for ballot; establish criteria for the geographical or jurisdictional distribution of signatures to ensure broad support; outline specific procedures to ensure due process; and, in some cases, limit the types of issues that can be determined in this manner. As a result of the changes that may accompany the widespread use of new technologies, these traditional safeguards are in jeopardy. Current standards for determining the validity of initiatives will therefore have to be reassessed in light of new technologies to ensure the present level of protections.

In particular, many experts are concerned about the need to promote the broader public interest and protect minority views against the potential abuses of unfettered majority rule. The potential speed with which initiatives could be generated and adopted in an electronic democracy raises a serious question as to whether such a process would ensure adequate discussion and deliberation among the electorate. In such an electronic republic, momentary passions or popular proposals could all too quickly be translated into initiatives or adopted in a referendum. Proposals could therefore qualify for the ballot or even be voted upon without a full debate or clear understanding of their merits or potential consequences.

More importantly, the legislative authority that such a process would place in the hands of a popular majority raises the issue of whether the rights of minorities would be adequately protected. As a number of conference members noted, the current system of representative government gives efficacy to minority views, often beyond the scope of their electoral strength, due to the bargaining and compromise that is required to form majority coalitions in legislative assemblies. If new technology does lead to more direct forms of election or governance, minority views may not be represented effectively and may become subject to the dictates of merely numerical popular majorities.

Any process of direct democracy then, should include safeguards to protect the polity from the potential abuses of direct majority rule. Rules will have to be adopted to uphold the integrity of the ballot, promote informed voter decision-making, ensure an adequate level of flexibility or revision, and protect both the public interest and minority views. Conference participants suggested a number of possible provisions that might help to secure these ends. These included: (1) a disclosure requirement that would ensure that voters were aware of the major sponsors/supporters of an initiative or referendum; (2) requirements governing the number of valid signatures needed to qualify an initiative for a vote, as well as provisions for a certain geographic or jurisdictional distribution to ensure broad support and acknowledgement of minority interests; (3) adoption of a "cooling off" or preliminary review period prior to the placement of an initiative on the ballot, during which time any initiative that had received an adequate level of support to qualify for the ballot would be subjected to public scrutiny, as well as judicial review; (4) procedures that would allow for some flexibility in the process, including a capacity to revise and amend the language of an initiative prior to any actual voting; (5) the possibility of a requirement that an initiative be approved twice, with some specified intervening period, before being adopted; and (6) if appropriate, a sunset provision to limit the duration of such proposals and provide an additional level of flexibility in the process.

CONCLUSION

For close to three decades the American political system has been characterized by increasing public disaffection and declining political participation. New technologies offer a means of reversing these trends. The interactive communication systems now being developed will provide individuals with powerful new means of accessing information and sharing their views with politicians and fellow citizens. They will offer citizens the opportunity to participate in elections and governance in meaningful ways, and could promote the type of interaction between voters and elected officials that is largely missing from modern politics. Eventually, they may lead to the creation of new forms of democratic participation that will supplement, or even replace, many of the representative structures that form the framework of our current constitutional system.

Emerging technologies thus offer the prospect of a revitalized democracy characterized by a more active and informed citizenry. But the realization of this promise will depend on whether all citizens can gain fair and equal access to the essential technologies. Another factor will be the extent to which policymakers successfully adapt current regulatory structures to accommodate new methods of communication. The most important factor, however, will be the willingness of significant numbers of citizens to take advantage of these extraordinary new tools to engage in meaningful political discourse, become better informed voters, and get more involved in civic life. If these technologies do stimulate greater public participation, then their impact may truly prove to be more revolutionary than that of radio and television.

Even if the problems of access and voter motivation can be overcome, the vision of an electronic democracy presents issues that will force us to rethink some of the basic foundations of our political system. One of the fundamental principles of our constitutional system is that popular opinion needs to be "filtered" through elected representatives in order to ensure proper deliberation and to protect the rights of minorities. Majority opinions can often represent momentary passions or popular ideas that may infringe on minority rights or entail consequences that would not be in the nation's long-term interest. Both our system of government and election laws are based on a scheme of checks and balances designed to prevent such consequences. But these checks could be undermined in an electronic republic.

In the *Federalist Papers*, James Madison warned of the dangers to free government posed by "factions," that is, groups of citizens motivated by particular interests rather than the public interest as a whole. One of the advantages of such a large country as ours, in his view, was that it inhibited individuals with "common motives" from organizing and acting on their personal interests due to the problems created by geographical distance and limited communications. These barriers have steadily eroded throughout this century and will be all but eliminated in an electronic republic. Emerging technologies will make it easy for individuals to transcend geographical barriers and organize in cyberspace with others who share their views. This will give rise to a plethora of interest groups or citizen movements that seek to influence electoral and legislative outcomes. Thus, instead of crystallizing majority views, technological innovation may increase the division of opinion throughout the nation and make consensus more difficult to achieve. This would further complicate voter decision-making, and make it harder to achieve the level of compromise needed to build electoral and legislative coalitions.

As one conference participant stated, the value of democracy is to be found in the civic virtue and civic spirit that it can instill in the citizenry. In the absence of these qualities, political participation produces at best a form of "vulgar democracy" in which individuals simply pursue their own self interests. Democratic governance then becomes an accumulation of independent efforts on the part of groups of individuals to fulfill their own interests, rather than a collective effort to achieve public goods. An effective democracy thus requires not just a need for better communications, but an increase in the amount of deliberation and debate that takes place within the citizenry. How to expand the arena of discourse and motivate citizens to capitalize on the variety of perspectives that will be available through new communications methods must therefore be a fundamental concern in the future development of technologies.

ENDNOTES

1. Robert H. Prisuta and Rebecca Sutterlin, *Personal Computers and Older Persons: Use and Ownership Trends and Projections* (Washington, DC.: American Association of Retired Persons, 1995), pp. 1–2.
2. Based on the findings of Jupiter Communications' 1996 Consumer On-line Services Report as reported in *USA Today,* April 30, 1996, p. 1D.
3. Rachel Van Dongen, "Buchanan Brigades Organize on the Net: Grassroots Go Online," *Roll Call,* March 11, 1996.
4. Michael Putzel, "Netting Votes: The Campaign Trail Merges with the Information Highway," *Boston Globe,* July 23, 1995, p. 63; and Jonathan Oatis, "White House Race Enters Cyberspace," Reuters News Service, February 19, 1996.
5. Graeme Browning, "Ballot Lines," *National Journal,* April 20, 1996, p. 880.
6. Ibid., p. 881.
7. Kevin Phillips, "Virtual Washington," *Time,* Spring 1995, p. 68.

Appendices

Assessing the Impact of New Technologies on the Political Process

by Sonia R. Jarvis

INTRODUCTION

I have been asked to offer my assessment of the impact communications and information technologies may have on the conduct of elections during the two election cycles following the current 1996 Presidential election process. My background includes grass roots community organizing, civil rights advocacy and litigation, political commentary, media and public policy analysis, and communications theory. By examining current social trends and the tenor of on-going political debates, this article will outline my expectations of how computers and new technologies will affect voter participation in the American democratic system. The resolution of competing interests through compromise is at the very heart of a democratic system of government. However, it is my thesis that current social and political trends indicate that conflict rather than compromise will be the nature of politics in the foreseeable future.

CURRENT SOCIAL TRENDS

In 1992, the nation witnessed, for the first time this century, that more votes were cast by residents living in suburban areas rather than by those living in cities. This shift was a reflection of the mass migration of middle class Americans from urban areas which began in the mid-1960s. While significant numbers of white Americans reacted to the desegregation of public school systems by fleeing central cities to the suburbs, the current trend of moving to the exurbs and beyond is more reflective of an avoidance of new waves of immigrants from Latin America, Asia, and the Middle East who are dominating metropolitan areas. This trend to "outmigrate" is complicated by issues such as the continued relative impoverishment of minority communities in urban areas, higher incidence of crime in cities, the desire for less stressful environments, and the decision by many corporations to relocate in more racially homogenous areas.

Moreover, white middle class Americans have been joined in this trend by their counterparts of other races. Unfortunately, suburban enclaves are as racially segregated as former inner city neighborhoods were before the civil rights movement. This movement of educated, economically secure citizens to a simpler and safer existence in racially homogenous areas has important consequences not only for what it represents in terms of basic civic interaction, but also what it means for the American political process. While the wish to live where others "look like you" can be explained as a desire to interact with others sharing common cultural values, what does that sentiment suggest about the status of a common culture that is shared by all Americans?

At precisely the same time the nation is becoming more ethnically diverse, Americans are choosing to live separate and apart from one another. Demographically speaking, in the next 25 years the nation may become divided into distinctly "ethno-cultural regions," according to the University of Michigan. With the country divided between whites living in exurbs and more rural areas west of Missouri, blacks living in major cities and the South, hispanics living in the Sunbelt states of Florida, Texas, New Mexico, and California, immigrants from Asia living in Hawaii and on the West Coast, and Native Americans on or near reservations in the Upper Midwest and West, how will it be possible for politicians to address issues on the national level much less govern effectively?

People who do not live in close proximity often do not have the opportunity to develop meaningful social relations that in turn can nurture a sense of common values. According to the *Washington Post*/Kaiser/Harvard survey:

America is becoming a nation of suspicious strangers, and this mistrust of each other is a major reason Americans have lost confidence in the federal government and virtually every other major national institution. Every generation that has come of age since the 1950s has been more mistrusting of human nature, a transformation in the national outlook that has deeply corroded the nation's social and political life.

In 1964, 76% of those surveyed agreed that the federal government in Washington could be trusted to do the right thing, whereas just 25% agreed in 1995. Similarly, 54% agreed that most people can be trusted, a figure that was only 35% in 1995.

Many organizations that depend upon the active participation of their members to exist have lamented the loss of a sense of community or common purpose. The Oxford English Dictionary defines community as "a body of people organized into a political, municipal, or social unity." The present pattern of suburbanization is one of the reasons this concept of community has faded. When people live in one place, work in another, go to school in yet a third, and perhaps shop and worship in a fourth location, a sense of loyalty to a single place necessarily fades and participation in daily aspects of civic life also declines. As a rule, Americans today are not joining groups, volunteering their time, or in general socializing to the degree that their parents and grandparents once did. Millions of Americans have withdrawn from the affairs of their communities since the mid-1970s, according to Robert Putnam of Harvard University.

This disengagement from public interaction or community life is one of the reasons voting and other forms of political involvement have declined dramatically in the last 30 years. While voting in presidential elections has declined by at least 10 percentage points between 1960 and 1992, the number of people during the past 20 years who participated in a political rally or speech declined 36 percent and those who actively worked for a political campaign declined 56 percent, according to the *Chicago Tribune*. As fewer people engage in political activity at the local level, politicians have

exacerbated the distance between themselves and potential supporters by curtailing face-to-face contacts in favor of messages
delivered electronically through television and more recently
through the Internet.

Recent surveys of American attitudes suggest that while many
Americans share the same concerns about the economy and the
future, they have been operating under misperceptions about
other ethnic groups that are often reflected in racially polarized
voting patterns. During a time of economic insecurity, we may
expect that politicians will continue to rely upon racially charged
rhetoric, stereotypes, and fears of "the other," that is until the
American electorate demonstrates that such tactics will not work.
Unfortunately, present housing patterns would indicate that such
appeals will continue to dominate political discussions to the
detriment of the nation as a whole. Scapegoating may offer short-
term benefits to a particular candidate, but it will ultimately inhibit
the nation's ability to face its real problems over the next decade.

Polarization is occurring not only with respect to racial and
ethnic identity but also with respect to other issues as well. The
"gender gap" in party identification at the national level, with
women favoring the Democrats and men favoring the Republicans,
can be expected to continue. Younger voters continue to demonstrate a declining interest in politics; anxiety over their future job
prospects has overridden normal activist behavior in the 18–24
year old cohort. Conversely, senior citizens continue to have the
highest voter turnout, a trend that should continue as the huge
"baby boom" generation ages and comes to understand the
importance of voting to securing retirement benefits. Current
debates over Medicare mask a deepening generational rift as the
baby boomers continue to age with a much smaller number of
workers to support present retirement policies.

POLITICAL TRENDS

One of the direct consequences of partisan bickering at the
national level is the effect it has had on the moderate wing of both
parties. The decision by an unprecedented number of moderate

Democrats and Republicans to decline to run for re-election to the U.S. Senate in 1996 is a harbinger of the deepening partisanship divide at the national level. As extremists from both sides of the aisle hone their appeals to their constituents, the majority of Americans who feel more comfortable somewhere in the middle will feel further disenfranchised. But without a strong candidate around whom to coalesce, the desire for the formation of a viable independent third party will remain just that.

There are a few indications that the American electorate will continue to accept divided government at the national level. Reaction against one party is immediately followed by the opposite reaction in the next election cycle. President Clinton's successful campaign as the first Democrat elected since the 1970s was followed by the total repudiation of the Democratic Party during the 1994 mid-term elections. The so-called "Republican Revolution" has been tempered by the sobering reality of completely shredding the complex set of social programs Americans have come to rely upon. Unusual coalitions have already formed at the national level over issues such as the environment and immigration. Others could argue with some support that Americans' rage at the status quo in Washington has reached its apex and that further disenchantment will depress voter turnout even more in the near future.

Thus it is very likely that control of the House of Representatives may fluctuate according to which party has control of the White House. On the other hand, it would appear that the Republicans will be able to maintain majority control of the Senate for the next two cycles as both a brake on the radicalism of the House Republicans and on the liberalism of the House when it was under Democratic control. The judiciary will continue to be conservative on balance and many public policies will be pro-business.

At the local level, Republicans will continue to enjoy majority control of statehouses for at least the next two election cycles. Republican governors have demonstrated a flexibility on social issues that has to date escaped the Republican majority in the House of Representatives. Yet Republican gubernatorial control could have important ramifications in the event that various Republican-sponsored constitutional amendments ever emerge from Congress.

Redistricting following the 2000 Census may be expected to produced heightened tensions over the ability of racial and ethnic minority groups to maintain any level of representation in state legislatures and in Congress. In view of the hostility the current majority on the Supreme Court has shown towards the Civil Rights Act and the Voting Rights Act, it is doubtful that race conscious policies within the political realm will survive into the next century. Many of the minority caucuses that formed in the early to mid-1970s will no longer be functionally active as the backlash against racially identifiable entities continues.

Money will continue to have a corrosive effect on the political process. Elections in 1994 and 1996 suggest that money alone will not determine the outcome of an election (e.g., Senate races in 1994; the Republican presidential nomination in 1996). However, the candidacies of Ross Perot and Steve Forbes at the presidential level and Oliver North and Michael Huffington at the Senate level demonstrate that money can dramatically affect the issues that dominate a primary or an election. Forbes in particular proved that the retail politics of the sort represented by the Iowa caucuses and the New Hampshire primary—namely face-to-face contact—is no longer a prerequisite to performing well in a primary. Any candidates with $10 million or more that they are willing to spend on television advertising can alter the field of a presidential election in ways not imaginable five years ago. In short, sound bites rather than substantive discussions of issues will be the rule rather than the exception.

Candidates are already utilizing television satellite technology to tailor their messages and their voting records to their constituents. Newspapers no longer have the budgets which allow reporters to follow candidates around as they meet with voters. Since many candidates have concluded that campaigning in person is less efficient, reporters will be able to track a campaign by downloading a politician's satellite feed. Radio hosts can dial in to "actualities," that is, taped quotes by a politician that can then be played over the radio. In 1996, politicians discovered the Internet and many created home pages on the World Wide Web, a trend that will definitely continue.

States will continue to experiment with ways to bring more voters to the polls or, increasingly, the polls to the voters. Missouri and Oregon have already allowed their citizens to vote by fax and by mail; Texas has utilized the "early vote" process which extends election day by two weeks. If the Rand Corporation is accurate in its assumption that one-half of American homes will be wired by the year 2000, then electronic voting is just around the corner. Once corporations figure out the best method for securing financial transactions on the Internet, it will only be a matter of time that the security and privacy issues associated with electronic voting will also be secured.

On balance, I favor any strategy that involves more people in the process. For example, I strongly supported the passage of the National Voter Registration Act which has already added over 11 million new voters since its implementation. But as expected, turnout in state and local races has yet to reflect these higher numbers of eligible voters. My major concern about new technologies that further remove citizens from human interaction while performing a basic duty like voting (namely casting a ballot in person) is that not all Americans will have equal access to the equipment and knowledge necessary to effectively use those modes of voting. Unlike television whose penetration includes even the poorest homes in America, computers are still relatively confined to middle and upper class homes. Even telephone service, which used to enjoy almost universal access, no longer reaches one out of four homes in urban areas due to increased costs. The growing gap between those who have access to information and equipment and those who do not will undoubtedly be a critical issue for this nation to confront in the decade ahead.

IMPACT OF TECHNOLOGY, INFORMATION ACCESS, AND THE MEDIA

I have been fascinated by the fact that as access to information increases exponentially, Americans in general appear to possess less knowledge about basic civic facts. Moreover, American children seem to possess less personal knowledge about history, civics, and geography. For example, the Washington Post/Kaiser/

Harvard survey indicated that only one in four American adults could correctly name their two senators. The survey notes that "knowing basic facts about politics does matter. The survey suggests that information is one of democracy's golden keys: Without basic facts about the players and the rules of the game, Americans tune out politics and turn off to voting."

Another survey, by the UCLA Higher Education Research Institute, reported that only 29 percent of college freshmen thought politics was important as compared to 58 percent in 1966. The academic achievement of American students has been described as lagging behind that of students from European and Asian nations, particularly with respect to math and science. If computer literacy replaces basic literacy as the lingua franca in the emerging global economy, the gap between information haves and have-nots will only widen over time.

One of the most exciting features of the Internet is its ability to connect people across barriers of age, sex, race, and other indicia of status. While membership in some traditional civics-minded groups has declined, there has been an explosion of interest in on-line activities and the formation of "virtual communities" as reflected in news groups, clubs that only meet on-line, and chat rooms. The question I am most concerned about is how can we guarantee that access to these new forms of communication will be available to every community that wants to participate?

When television was first promoted, its developers empha-sized the ability of the new technology to educate and unify communities. Television remains a vital component of the new information technologies, and new distance learning programs developed by community colleges demonstrate the potency of television's ability to educate. However, we have also seen its ability to anesthetize the people who watch hours of television and thereby undermine the political process. According to Putnam, television viewing has eroded not only volunteerism but also newspaper reading: each hour spent watching television leads to less social trust and less group membership, while each hour reading newspapers is associated with more. Moreover, the loss of face-to-face contact within the context of a political campaign is a trend that began with the advent of television coverage of political campaigns in the early 1960s, the high watermark of political participation for the second half of this century.

We will see some combination of a television, telephone, and computer in the near future on which local, national, and international communication will be possible with a keystroke. News is no longer the sole province of those who own printing presses or broadcast licenses, so in that sense computers support democracy at its most basic level. Yet at the same time, the power underlying processes which allow people to watch television or place a call or access a computer network is being consolidated in fewer and fewer hands which may ultimately threaten true access to free speech and new ideas. The greater access to information technologies has also generated a backlash in the form of increased censorship and surveillance (e.g., the "clipper chip" and wiretaps of computer e-mail accounts) by the government. Once voting, the most basic right fundamental to all other rights we enjoy as citizens, becomes subject to the control of those few who own the airwaves, cable lines, or satellites, the viability of American democracy itself will be at risk without careful diligence on the part of the very citizens who have expressed a lack of interest in public affairs.

CONCLUSION

While there are many reasons for serious concerns about the next decade, there are an equal number of reasons for optimism about our nation's prospects. The threat of nuclear annihilation has diminished significantly, the environment is in better shape than it was 20 years ago, and communication technology has brought the world closer together. Race relations, while still strained, are certainly better than they were 40 years ago, and I expect the black middle class to continue to grow and develop in the near term. Immigration has been a net plus for the nation despite any discomfort it may have caused on the social level. And certainly the status of women is better than it was a generation ago in many (though not all) important respects.

In addition, some Americans have responded to problems at the local level, which provides me with hope that the spirit of community which formerly defined this nation can be revived. Information technologies can further this budding movement by connecting small groups of people around the country. Churches and religious organizations are enjoying an increase in membership suggesting another means of connecting citizens to work on behalf of the common good rather than from a parochial basis. Schools, public libraries, and hospitals, if they receive the proper funding and support, can serve as the starting point for resource-poor communities and individuals.

Thus, in many significant ways, America continues to have the possibility of a bright future. Immigration, legal or illegal, would otherwise not be a problem if people from other countries did not want to live and work here. The challenge ahead is whether the widening economic, social, and technological gaps—between the rich and poor, the current majority and people of color, those with access to information and those without—will transform the promise of the American experiment in democratic government into a failure. Communications technologies will have a vital role in answering that question.

REFERENCES

_____. *The Freedom Forum Media Studies Journal,* 9, No. 3 (1995).

Barone, Michael. "The Road Back to Tocqueville—At Last, 19th Century Values Stage a Revival," *Washington Post,* January 7, 1996, p. C1.

Belluck, Pam. "In Era of Shrinking Budgets, Community Groups Blossom," *New York Times,* February 25, 1996, p. A1.

Berke, Richard L. "The Mellowing of The American Voter," *New York Times,* January 7, 1996, p. E1.

Biskupic, Joan. "Court Won't Hear State Challenge to 'Motor Voter' Law," *Washington Post,* January 23, 1996, p. A1.

Brodie, Mollyann. "The Four Americas: Government, and Social Policy Through the Eyes of America's Multi-racial and Multi-ethnic Society: A Report of the *Washington Post*/Kaiser Family Foundation, Harvard Survey Project," December 1995.

Egan, Timothy. "Oregon's Mail-In Election Brings Cheers for Clinton and Democrats," *New York Times,* February 1, 1996, p. A1.

Glaberson, William. "Newspaper Owners Do the Shuffle—Communities Worry as Dailies Pass from Chain to Chain," *New York Times,* February 19, 1996, p. D1.

Hardwood, Richard. "People Behind the Numbers," *Washington Post,* February 23, 1996, p. A19.

Kolbert, Elizabeth. "TV Is Changing the Script For Early Political Races," *New York Times,* February 11, 1996, p. A1.

Kotkin, Joel. "White Flight to the Fringes," *Washington Post,* March 10, 1996, p. C1.

Lewis, Charles. *The Buying of the President* (New York: Avon Books, 1996).

Miller, Judith. "America's Burden: At Hour of Triumph, Democracy Recedes as the Global Ideal," *New York Times,* February 18, 1996, p. A19.

Raspberry, William. "Why We're Losing Sight of the Common Good," *Washington Post,* February 23, 1996, p. A19.

Campaign 2000:
A Scenario

by Jeffrey Abramson

In developing a scenario for the presidential election of 2000, I have made the following assumptions:

- The "motor voter" registration law succeeds in substantially increasing the number of registered voters but not the number of actual voters. Turnout remains around 55% for the 2000 election.[1]

- States supplement motor voter registration with other schemes, for example, permitting college students to register to vote alongside registering for classes.[2]

- Candidates manage to obtain registration lists that indicate who is a motor voter registrant, a student registrant, or a traditional registrant. They conduct their direct-mail campaigns accordingly.

- VCRs continue to be the fastest growing new communications device since color television. Abroad, in closed societies, they remain an important method of oppositional politicking. In the United States, candidates distribute videocassettes but they have no serious political impact on voters.

- Fax machines come down in price and achieve rapid home penetration. Candidates use faxes not only to rally the committed but to communicate with undecided voters.

- Likewise, electronic mail has sufficient market penetration to become an important form of direct mail campaigning, at phenomenally low cost.

- Apart from e-mail, however, the Internet does not emerge as an important campaign forum in 2000. I assume that the number of persons with access to the Internet has vastly increased by 2000 and that by then traditional long-distance telephone providers have positioned themselves to be the primary Internet connection providers, with something like a universal dial tone for all information services. In regard to classroom, educational, and commercial uses, the Internet has come of age by 2000, and yet campaign uses lag far behind. Television is still clearly the medium of choice not only because it reaches a vastly greater audience, but also because it reaches an accidental audience that would not purposely watch political programming. By contrast, candidates find that partisan voters make use of the Internet but that undecideds do not yet feel comfortable with the "unfiltered" nature of Internet information.

- Out of necessity, third party candidates in 2000 will pioneer uses of Internet and e-mail campaigning. Indeed, the relatively low cost of reaching voters and soliciting funds by credit card over computers permits third parties to solve some of the problems of ballot access and money that have always doomed third party candidacies in the past.

- Although the Internet does not emerge as a direct tool of campaigning, it still has tremendous political impact. The impact centers on economic dislocations caused by continued downsizing and merger-driven consolidations—dislocations that bring employment concerns home to roost for middle class managers. As the great American historian Richard Hofstadter traced out, large-scale shifts in the nature of work trigger a "paranoid style" in American politics, as real and perceived insecurities make people ripe for "populist" appeals for a return to the passing economic order and for immigration and trade restrictions that will allegedly save jobs. At the same time, if the Hofstadter cycle holds true, a more "progressive" party will also rise, which accepts the new economy and relies on government regulation to tame the fears.

- The Supreme Court revisits First Amendment restrictions on campaign finance reform and decides, partly overruling *Buckley v. Valeo*, that ceilings on campaign expenditures are constitutional, as applied both to a candidate's own money and to so-called independent expenditures by a political action committee not controlled by the candidate. This solves the so-called Forbes advantage under current election law.

Early in 1997, former New Jersey Senator Bill Bradley approaches General Colin Powell and suggests that the two join forces to launch a third-party bid for the presidency in 2000. Offering to be Powell's vice presidential running mate, Bradley points to exit polls conducted on Election Day 1996, which showed Powell handily defeating either major party presidential candidate.

Before making his decision, Powell studies the results of a computer simulation designed to show whether an African-American man who favors affirmative action and freedom of choice on abortion can win the Republican Party nomination. These simulations have improved markedly by 2000. Popular among younger voters already at home with computer games, they give new meaning to voter rationality by permitting participants to play out options, make trade-offs, and see the consequences of their choices. Still, direct political uses of such simulations are rare—their primary use remains in secondary schools, where higher income school districts use computers to teach students problem-solving skills (although a surface parity exists between rich and poor school districts in terms of computer access, the actual instruction differs, with poorer districts employing computers mostly to help with basic skills learning).

After studying the results of his simulated run in the Republican primaries, Powell accepts Bradley's offer to become the presidential candidate of the newly formed Progressive Party. With moderates siphoned off by the Powell candidacy, Pat Buchanan has little trouble winning the Republican Party nomination. More surprising is former New York Governor Mario Cuomo's Lazarus-like return from the political dead to capture the Democratic Party nomination.

The immediate task of the Progressive Party is to qualify for ballot access in all 50 states and to solicit campaign funds. The gathering of sufficient signatures to qualify for the ballot in any one state is greatly facilitated by e-mail, faxes, and web pages on the Internet carrying instructions, information, and legal requirements for mounting a ballot petition drive. Cost for a web site, which was approximately $1,000 a month during the 1996 primaries, is now half that sum. In October 1995, only 5.8 million American adults had direct access to the Internet. That number more than doubled to 12 million by the end of the 1996 election year and by some estimates surpassed 40 million in January of 1999.[3] Moreover, according to a 1995 study by The Times Mirror Center for The People and The Press, a majority of those buying home computers earn less than $50,000 a year. These trends encourage all three parties to place new reliance on the Internet. But the third-party effort of Powell and Bradley, strapped for money and needing to gather signatures quickly in order to qualify for the ballot, makes most use of the Internet.

Early on, the new party seeks to have election commissions in several states accept electronic signatures on computer-generated ballot petitions. But they abandon this effort after failing to offer any way of verifying the electronic "signatures." Still, the Progressive Party uses e-mail to good effect to alert people to its ballot petition drive. Moreover, e-mail seems to have revived the epistolary instinct of Americans and supported virtual communities of conversation about social and political issues. The task of launching a third party is made that much easier by such associations of like-minded Americans. Indeed, the Progressive Party studies the highly successful use Ralph Nader's Green Party made of the Internet and e-mail in 1996 in gaining access to the presidential ballot in California. Exposure on California's on-line service, The Democracy Network, also helped launch the Green Party at low cost, and the Progressive Party follows suit in using these relatively low cost ways of reaching voters.

In states such as Florida, which permit college students over eighteen to register to vote in conjunction with registering for classes, the Progressive Party makes a targeted effort to reach these new registrants with its ballot petition drives. However, legal challenges proliferate as to whether many of Florida's two million college students met residency requirements for registering to vote in that state.

All is not pretty on the Internet, however. Efforts to sabotage the fledgling Progressive Party include fake, look-alike web pages set up by political enemies. Moreover, there are almost no restraints on negative campaigning over the Internet, and false and defamatory charges about all three candidates are rampant: you can read about Cuomo's alleged Mafia connections, Buchanan's alleged membership in the American Nazi Party, and belated news about how Bill Bradley allegedly cooperated with gamblers in a point-shaving operation while a basketball player at Princeton University. Since most of the libelous remarks are posted anonymously, candidates threaten to sue the various bulletin boards or on-line services for publishing or republishing the libels but these are empty threats.

In attempts to swell its list of e-mail addresses, the Committee to Elect Buchanan (CEB) buys names of subscribers from America Online, CompuServe, and Prodigy. Those services had previously agreed to inform subscribers that they sold subscriber lists to third parties and to provide subscribers with an opportunity to "opt out" of inclusion on such lists of names for sale. But practically speaking, the opt-out choice is not noticed by most subscribers and many now find themselves unwilling recipients of CEB mail. To make matters worse, the Cuomo Election Committee (CEC) charges that these same on-line services refused to sell it a similar list of subscriber names. The services deny the charge; meanwhile, CEC turned to a private company, Venture, which specializes in offering free gifts to persons over the Internet, compiling names, addresses and other information about respondents, and selling lists containing this information. The Cuomo campaign is hurt when news of its use of the Venture front becomes known.

The Progressive Party turns to soliciting contributions over the Internet, including taking credit card contributions by secure computer. After some doubts, the Federal Election Commission (FEC) approves such solicitations, so long as appropriate computer and paper records of contributions are kept and so long as the solicitation informs persons that "federal election law prohibits contributions from foreign nationals who do not have permanent resident status." The FEC deems this warning necessary, since Internet solicitations are more likely to reach foreign nationals than are conventional ways of soliciting contributors.

Despite the warning, some Japanese and Korean corporations, fearful of Buchanan's protectionist politics, make contributions to the Progressive Party in only slightly detoured ways. Buchanan seizes on this news to fire up his Japan-bashing campaign rhetoric. Militia groups, with their own home pages and lines of electronic communication, pick up on the Buchanan rhetoric—which leads Cuomo to denounce Buchanan as in league with the militia movement. Meanwhile, the armed forces have been monitoring the e-mail comings and goings of enlisted men and women and move to discharge any one who has sent or received mail to a militia group. Indeed, as recommended by a 1996 task force, the armed forces now ask potential recruits whether they belong to or receive communications from any "extremist" organizations (potential recruits are provided with a list of extremist organizations). Citing free speech concerns, the American Civil Liberties Union files suit on behalf of one potential recruit rejected by the Army after the recruit acknowledged having signed on to read the home page of the Montana Militia.

Media sources begin to monitor the free trade/protectionist debate. Unfortunately, ABC, NBC, and CBS have abandoned the traditional nightly news format by 2000—declining ratings, loss of market share, and an inability to rival the timeliness of CNN were cited as reasons. In place of news, the big three networks each offer an hour long newsmagazine each night during prime time modeled after "Dateline NBC." However, these programs largely ignore the presidential election in favor of recapping the day's top story out of the O.J. Simpson civil trial, entering its fifth year in 2000.

Still, there are plenty of media watchdogs. Public television continues to experiment with the electronic town meeting format and the deliberative poll—convening representative groups of Americans to see if initial opinions on the free trade debate change once participants have an opportunity to swap views with others and to participate in question and answer sessions with leading economists. In devising its new interactive programming, PBS is influenced by a number of sources: the work of University of Texas political scientist James Fishkin on deliberative polls and the need to combine civic education with poll taking; the 1996 blockbuster books on democracy by Harvard political scientists Michael Sandel and Robert Putnam, both of whom show that democracy depends on a rich pattern of civic associations where people learn a sense of community and the habits of talking politics with others; and the work of the Aspen Institute on developing standards for electronic town meetings that would make the meetings truly interactive, free from fraud and manipulation, and not just platforms for candidates to "work" the audience à la Oprah Winfrey.

The problem that surfaces in 2000 is that the media simply are not equipped to be responsible, as an institution, for convening Americans into the modern equivalent of old-style civic associations. It is one thing for people to form a community and to debate that community's needs when their real lives bring them together in the workplace, neighborhood associations, churches, synagogues, mosques, interfaith councils, Rotary Clubs, and parent-teacher organizations. It is quite another for television to gather essentially isolated individuals for a one-shot deliberative exercise—such people can hardly display the same concern for one another's welfare that people do when they share a community. Campaign 2000 makes clear that, although democracy does indeed depend on deliberation preceding voting, technology alone cannot create common communities of interest.

By default, then, Election 2000 falls back on television advertising as the principal way of appealing to voters—a way that permits the candidate to speak one-on-one to individuals in the privacy of their homes. For all the attempts to "recongregate" citizens in virtual communities on the Internet or in televised town meetings, the election still turns on television's ability to give individuals the illusion of personally meeting the candidate.

But there are some important differences between the ad campaign of 2000 and the ad campaigns of 1996. Empirical studies of Steve Forbes' run for the Republican nomination in 1996 show that he sank like a stone when his ad campaign became almost exclusively negative; this moderates the tone of the 2000 ads. The Powell/Bradley ads center on war as basketball and basketball as war—staying away from issues in favor of delivering to voters the simple message that these are persons you can trust.

Buchanan's ad strategy is complicated by the three-way race: polls pick up such great volatility in the electorate that it remains unclear whether the Progressive Party is appealing to traditional Democratic or Republican voters. The best advice is that Buchanan should solidify his hold on blue-collar, Reagan Democrats. He attempts to do this with gritty realist ads that picture factories moving abroad and workers losing their jobs. The controversial feature of his ads is a reference to a web site where viewers can play a simulation game to see whether a Powell or Cuomo victory would threaten their own job.

Cuomo alone eschews a big-budget television ad campaign. Confident in his stump speech ability, he barnstorms the country, with a standard speech that says it is time for Democrats to offer a moral vision for the nation, but a moral vision that is inclusive rather than exclusive and that builds on the core notion that we are one community that houses many communities. In line with the content of his speech, Cuomo seeks a diversity of venues—inner city, ethnic, religious, labor. He can count on attracting free television time and is the candidate most aware that the abundance of channel capacity, the arrival of cable as a player, and the existence of CNN means that there is a surplus of television time to be lavished freely on the campaign.

By Labor Day 2000, tracking polls show the Powell/Bradley ticket in the lead but splitting votes with Cuomo in a way that keeps Buchanan in the race. Advisers urge the Powell forces to go negative in their ad campaigns on Cuomo. Stay tuned.

ENDNOTES

1. B. Drummond Ayres, Jr., "Easier Voter Registration Hasn't Raised Participation," *The New York Times*, Dec. 3, 1995, sec. 1, p. 22.
2. "Florida May Take Motor Voter Step Further," *The New York Times*, Feb. 25, 1996, p. 19.
3. Eleanor Randolph, "GOP Field is At Home on the Web," *The Los Angeles Times*, Oct. 27, 1995, p. A1.

2004:
A Digital Election Scenario

by Tracy Westen

November 2002, Pre-Election: The next Presidential election—
a mere two years away in 2004—is beginning to heat up.

The regional Western States Presidential Primary Election, only
eleven months off, is scheduled for October 2003, to be followed
over the next few months by regional primaries in the Midwestern
States, the Atlantic States and the Southern States' "Super Tuesday."

Candidate fundraising is already in full swing. "Sim-Election
2004" has appeared in software stores and is down-loadable via
high-speed cable modems—allowing you to play a simulated
game of "select the next president" on your computer. Candidate
World Wide Web pages are up and multiplying. And your e-mail
is filling up with a series of political public opinion polls—all
offering you a $25 credit if you "spend only a few minutes
answering these important questions."

Most indicative of the season, political commercials are beginning to appear on your customized on-line computer screen saver
and in programs on your GTE cable television system.

You're watching TV and are a little surprised when Jane Smith,
a Democratic candidate for president, addresses you by name in
her 30-second cable commercial. "John," she says in a serious
tone, "I need your vote in the Western States Democratic Presidential Primary. I share your concerns over jobs being exported
overseas, women's right to choose, the need for stronger environmental protections, and the importance of a constitutional
amendment to allow mandatory campaign expenditure ceilings in

political races. With your help, I will work to makes these vital goals a reality."

It takes you a moment to remember that computer selected and assembled "addressable" campaign ads can now be tailored to individual cable television households. Candidate consultants run cross-checks on your political party registration, magazine subscriptions, organizational memberships and patterns of campaign contributions. Any candidate with up-to-date research capabilities can come close to determining your positions on specific issues. You wonder, however, if candidate Smith's cable television ads are saying the same thing to your more conservative next-door neighbors.

You have read that, in the near future, political candidates and elected officials will be able to place computer-generated images of themselves into interactive television systems, using technology which first came to public attention in the classic 1990s films, *Terminator II* and *Jurassic Park*. These computer-generated images will appear on your television set, address you by name and deliver speeches, present news conferences, and answer your constituent mail ("Well, John, I'm glad you're home this evening. I thought I'd explain to you my new flat tax proposal . . .").

As an "early adopter," you have one of the new high-definition, flat screen, digital television sets which combine the features of the older analog sets (large screens, remote control viewing, access to high-quality movies and other programming) and personal computers (sharper screen, full two-way interactivity, user access to digital programming in a text, voice or video format). You've also subscribed to GTE Cable's "Full Service Network," which gives you high-speed access to a full range of digitized video Web sites. (You smile when you remember your first 14,400 bits-per-second modem, which you purchased in 1995; your cable modem now delivers 10 million bits-per-second.) You can use your remote control (or "air mouse") to select digitized video programming from a vast menu of programs. GTE's central "server" (or mainframe computer) contains video selections in a digitized format and delivers them to you on request.

You've also invested in a small $50 TV camera, no bigger than a walnut, which sits atop your television set. You typically use this for video teleconferencing from your living room, but you can also record short video statements and transmit them, like e-mail, to GTE's central server, which stores them and makes them available to others who want to know your views. As a senior partner in one of the nation's larger virtual accounting firms, your views are respected by thousands of your younger associates who know of your reputation—and your progressive views. As a courtesy to them, you place your video views on issues in GTE's public file, making them accessible to all who wish to view them.

A lot has happened since 1995, you reflect. Although not widely recognized at the time, 1995 was the year of the "great digital phase shift." That year, for the first time, personal computers outsold television sets; the number of e-mail messages surpassed surface mail messages; and data traffic over telephone networks (driven by an amazing increase in Internet usage) exceeded voice traffic. Students now study 1995 as the year which marked the true beginning of the "Digital Age."

The morning surface mail arrives. You flip through an assortment of campaign mailers, free videocassettes from various candidates, ballot initiative petitions and CD-ROMs with a selection of candidate "slates" and issues. You toss out the fundraising solicitations—it's too early for you to make a contribution. Solicitations are filling your e-mail system, too. You set your VCR-plus to pick up short satellite-delivered video clips from candidates with pro-environmental views. You'll watch them later. You wish political campaigns wouldn't start so early.

November 2003, Ballot Initiative Circulation: The election is still a year away, but there is an important matter you have to attend to. You turn on your home/office computer, go to the Internet, and click *The Democracy Network* icon. *The Democracy Network* is a system of free, on-line, voter information, a "digital C-SPAN" available over the Internet and supported by a consortium of communications industries, including computer manufacturers, software companies, and telephone companies. You click "California Ballot Initiatives in Circulation." Deadlines are approaching for ballot initiative qualification, and you want to make sure your favorites are among them.

In California, ballot initiatives have been steadily increasing in number. Between the 1960s and 1970s, the number of initiatives reaching the ballot tripled; they doubled again in the 1980s; and since then they have continued to increase. Since 1990, more money has been spent lobbying the California public to vote on ballot initiatives than has been spent lobbying all of state government to vote on legislation. There may be over 30 citizen-drafted initiatives on the November 2004 ballot.

You read a list of short ballot initiative summaries, click various icons, see video statements from the proponents and opponents of those initiatives, check Ralph Nader's opposition to the six "no-fault" insurance initiatives being circulated, and call up the "signature screen." You decide not to sign any of the three "right-to-life" anti-abortion initiatives, but you support an initiative making California an "ozone-free zone," one requiring out-of-door cigarette smokers to use portable "emission control devices," and one protecting California sea urchins from over fishing. You consider supporting measures expanding the sales tax from tangible property to services and converting the state legislature into a unicameral body, but you decide you don't know enough about their consequences and pass.

You spend some time thinking about a controversial initiative which would create a new process of electronic ballot initiative qualification. If enacted, it would allow proponents to circulate their ballot initiatives electronically via the Internet. This would greatly reduce the time and cost of ballot initiative qualification—enabling lower income groups to circulate their initiatives as easily as well-heeled organizations. (You're aware that wealthy organizations are increasingly dominating the initiative process itself—since the 1980s, the 20 highest-spending ballot initiatives in California have raised two-thirds of all their funding in contribution amounts of $100,000 or more and one-third of all their funding in contribution amounts of $1 million or more.) You decide to support this electronic initiative qualification measure.

As a heavy computer user (in 2003, for the first time, the average person began to spend more hours in front of a computer screen than in front of a television set), you are frustrated by ballot initiatives that take over a year to circulate, qualify, and appear on the ballot. By then, the problems the initiatives were designed to solve have become worse. You want the ability to respond more quickly to the state's problems. Despite the recent advertising blitz against so-called "instant initiatives," conducted by incumbent state legislators and large political action committees, you want to see this electronic initiative qualification measure appear on the ballot. You click the appropriate icons and electronically add your Personal Identification Number, digital signature, and address to the selected initiative petitions.

Of course, all these initiative campaigns want money. You check the appropriate icons and contribute $25 to each of the initiative campaigns you support. Your funds are transferred electronically. Frustrated by the reluctance of incumbent legislators to adopt campaign finance reforms, the creators of *The Democracy Network* have installed built-in campaign contribution limits. They prevent you from contributing more than $25 to any initiative or candidate for office. Candidates voluntarily agreeing to abide by campaign expenditure ceilings, however, can receive larger contributions—up to $100 per contributor.

In the 1990s, many campaign finance reform organizations sought to persuade state legislatures and the Congress to limit the amounts of money candidates could raise and spend. The growth of computer-assisted campaign contributions, however, radically changed campaign financing patterns. Instead of receiving the bulk of their funding from large donors, candidates and ballot measure committees began to raise tens of thousands of small ($5 and $10) contributions over the Internet. Responding to the pleas of reformers, software developers began to build campaign finance reforms into their programs.

You check your computer screen. These initiatives have only been in circulation for about a week, yet they have each already received over one million signatures and $2 million in contributions. They'll be certain to qualify for the ballot in November 2004. Fortunately, voters recently adopted a ballot initiative to reform the ballot initiative process itself. Now, all initiatives qualified electronically can be unilaterally modified by their proponents—after qualification, but before the election—to correct inadvertent drafting errors. The initiatives themselves, however, must be approved by a simple majority of all voters in two successive elections. That will give you a chance to rethink your vote if you decide you've made a mistake.

October 2004, Voter Education: The election is now only a month away. You need to begin your voter education effort. You will have over 200 individual ballot decisions to make, including decisions on 35 ballot measures, additional choices for local, appellate, and supreme court judges, and decisions on a host of new state offices, including environmental commissioner, transportation commissioner, political-reform commissioner, gay rights commissioner, air pollution commissioner, drug commissioner, telecommunications commissioner, and child-abuse commissioner. It's time to get started.

You settle down on your couch, pick up your television set's remote control, and speak the word "menu" into it. Most television remotes now come with built-in microphones, which provide voice-recognition access to any menu item on your system. Your Southwestern Bell Communications Cable System is increasingly voice-driven, a substantial convenience. (During the past year, GTE sold its cable system to Southwestern Bell Communications, giving SBC, with its 1996 acquisition of Pacific Telesis, substantial control over California's telephone and video market.) You ask for *The Democracy Network* and settle back for an evening's work.

The Democracy Network is a non-profit, voter information service available over computers and interactive digital television systems. It is keyed to your Personal Identification Number and nine-digit zip code. It displays all the candidates and ballot measures on your local ballot—including city council candidates, county supervisors, judges, regional officials, state legislators, and federal candidates. You skip the presidential candidates—you've decided against voting for incumbent President Al Gore, Republican challenger Newt Gingrich or perennial Green Party candidate Ralph Nader. This time you're going to vote for Bill Gates, the independent candidate running under the banner of Ross Perot's United We Stand Party.

You ask *The Democracy Network* to start by displaying information on the "Governor's race." *The Democracy Network* offers you a wide selection of video materials on all the gubernatorial candidates, divided into four categories:

- video statements and other materials completely controlled, prepared, and edited by the candidates themselves;

- materials prepared and inserted by local television and radio stations and newspapers, including news coverage of the candidates, news interviews, and digitized candidate debates (allowing viewers to select from an index of topics and view only the portion of the debate they want to see);

- opinions on the gubernatorial candidates from statewide organizations (Common Cause, Rock the Vote, California Taxpayers Association); and

- opinions on the candidates by individual members of the public, whose views are organized and appear by topic.

These options are offered through a lengthy sub-menu of video materials, including:

- opening candidate "vision" statements;

- candidate statements on over 30 specific issues (e.g., crime, immigration, health care, environment, schools, local taxation, air pollution, jobs, the economy, welfare)—in the future, you'll be able to compare the candidates' statements with their statements on the same issues in prior elections;

- candidate positions endorsing or opposing the 35 initiative measures on the ballot;

- video endorsements by supporters of the candidates;

- news clips on the candidates dating back six months;

- news interviews with the candidates;

- newspaper editorials from across the state, organized by locality;

- biographical material on the candidates;

- opinions of state organizations and individual citizens for and against the various candidates;

- questions of the candidates by organizations and citizens, followed by the candidates' digitized video answers;

- live candidate forums, in which viewers can ask video teleconferenced questions of candidates and receive direct answers, all of which can be watched by anyone with access to *The Democracy Network*;

- television, radio, and print ads by all the candidates, organized by topic; and

- campaign finance information, listing all the candidates' contributors over the past two years and highlighting major donors (giving over $10,000).

All of this material, of course, is available in Spanish, Chinese, Korean, Japanese, Farsi, and Tagalog, with subtitles and voice-overs supplied by the candidates using politically neutral translation agencies. You choose English.

You sigh at the sheer quantity of this available material and wish that Southwestern Bell's new *"Smart Agent"* was available (its scheduled release won't occur until 2006). Then, you'll be able to program your political views into your system, and your *Smart Agent* will preliminarily select all those candidates and ballot measures which agree most closely with your opinions. Until then, you've got to do it all yourself. You review the candidate "endorsements," "campaign contributions" and positions on "environmental" issues—those are the most important, in your view.

As you work your way through the dozens of ballot choices, you periodically use your remote control to mark your electronic sample ballot. There are so many choices that you may forget your early decisions by the time you reach the end of the ballot. The cable system's computer remembers your choices; when you're finished, it prints out a sample ballot individualized with your choices for you to take to the polls.

Even this seems ridiculously slow. You've heard that in the next election, *The Democracy Network* will allow you to obtain an absentee ballot via your television set or computer. You'll simply print it out in your home, fill it out, and mail it in. In future elections, you will be able to take a digitized version of your filled-in ballot to the polls with you. There, you'll simply upload it into the precinct's computer—saving you the time of laboriously having to punch out your ballot candidate-by-candidate and issue-by-issue.

To your relief, you hear that electronic voting is finally just around the corner. This technology, which will allow voters to use their computers and television sets to mark and electronically transmit their votes and ballots from their homes, has been available for several years, but politicians have blocked its implementation. They *say* they're concerned over "electronic vote tampering"—a husband voting for his wife, or a computer hacker breaking into the mainframe and altering the vote totals. But most political experts believe that incumbent politicians fear a diminution of their power—through the growth of minority political parties and the increase in "instant ballot initiatives," measures which can be electronically circulated, qualified, and approved within a matter of weeks.

That reminds you to check the ballot measure section of *The Democracy Network*. You review the pro and con statements for the measures on which you are still undecided, check Common Cause's position on each, view some of the television ads for each measure, watch the *Sacramento Bee's* political reporter critique each ad for accuracy, and mark your sample ballot.

You decide to vote for one "no-fault" insurance initiative (that should drive the final stake through the heart of the trial lawyers' lobby), against the six "right-to-life" anti-abortion initiatives, for restrictions on outdoor smoking, and for sea urchins over commercial fishermen. You also decide it's time to expand the state's tax base and extend the sales tax to services—that should create more funding for public schools. And you vote to convert the state to one with a unicameral legislature—why pay for two houses of legislators when they don't do much anyway?

Most importantly, you decide to vote for the initiative allowing future circulation and qualification of ballot measures electronically. If it passes, initiative proponents can draft and qualify their initiatives for the ballot within a matter of weeks—without massive volunteer efforts or paid signature gatherers. You've even heard talk that, if this initiative passes, a future initiative will be circulated to allow initiatives to be voted on within a few weeks after their qualification. After all, if policy crises arise in the state and the legislature refuses to act (legislative logjams and political stalemates seem to be occurring more and more often these days), then the people should be able to vote quickly—without waiting almost two years before the next election. Besides, it's too confusing to have to vote on 35 initiatives in one election. Why not spread them out and vote on them monthly?

You stop for a moment and think about the most troubling initiative: an advisory measure that would ask your U.S. Senator and Member of Congress to support a constitutional amendment modifying Article 5 of the U.S. Constitution. Article 5 currently guarantees to every state a republican form of government—a government of elected representatives (not a governmental "majority of Republicans," as one wag recently remarked). In light of rapid advances in digital technology, it is increasingly clear that many states are moving toward new hybrid forms of "direct democracy," bypassing elected representatives and allowing the people to vote directly on important state measures via computers and interactive television systems.

Legislative incumbents have threatened litigation, contending that the growth of electronic ballot initiatives is inconsistent with Article 5 and is undermining the nation's system of legislative checks and balances. The Cyber-Rights Foundation has circulated an initiative proposing language which would amend Article 5. This language would make it clear that states can substitute forms of direct democracy for their current systems of representative democracy, if they choose.

State legislatures seem to be fighting more and doing less these days—acting more like honorary bodies, such as the British House of Lords, and leaving the real legislation to the people. It seems the trend toward "democracy by initiative" is inevitable. Of course, legislators don't like losing their power. But they only have themselves to blame.

You decide to support the initiative. Why fight progress?

Author's Note: Most of the technologies referenced in this article already exist. A few are yet to be put in place, although they have been described and predicted.

Voting, Campaigns, and Elections in the Future: Looking Back From 2008

by Nolan A. Bowie

When the Director of The Aspen Institute's Communications and Society Program, Charles Firestone, first asked me to consider writing a scenario on the future of political campaigns and elections in the United States, he concluded our conversation by cheerfully commenting: "Just use the best of your *pessimistic views* when you explore the possibilities. We're looking for a paper that will stimulate discussion." "Great," I thought, "this should be an easy assignment."

I anticipate continuing, rapidly changing information technology and large doses of uncertainty concerning the emerging, evolving, knowledge-based, global economy. In the long term, I expect that these changes ultimately threaten not only the United States as an independent sovereign, but the very concept of the nation-state and democracy.[1] In the following view of science fiction, I am guided by current significant trends regarding campaigns, elections, and voting patterns in the United States.[2]

I begin my scenario in the year 2008 and look back, describing some of the significant pessimistic circumstances surrounding the general elections of the years 2000 and 2004 that got us to that glorious point in time, 2008, when the demand for democratic reform was manifest—a time in *forehistory* when all good citizens took to the public sphere[3] and knowingly reclaimed their government and its infrastructure (commonwealth) for themselves and their common interests (also known as "the public interest"), as they believed they were mandated to do under the U.S. Declaration of Independence. In other words, in the year 2008, a nation of viewers and consumers finally took the step to act as *citizens.*

What moved the people towards dramatic political reform was the intervening presidential elections of four and eight years earlier. Those were the years of "bad campaigns" for citizens—that is to say, campaigns that did not inform or motivate them into action. Conversely, those were the years of "good campaigns" for the candidates, candidates' spin doctors and consultants, political pundits, pollsters, and the television station owners that reaped between 70 and 80 percent of candidates' campaign expenditures in exchange for a little access to the public's airwaves.

I create a "worst world" scenario (in the best of my pessimistic nature) in order to conclude with the optimistic hope of saving democracy. The common denominator of both worlds is ubiquitous information technology. The difference is information and choice—information that is relevant and accessible to citizens. In the best world, citizens are informed and empowered to make political choices about issues affecting the daily lives of all the people. In the worst world, wealth and power are synonymous and "corporate citizens" determine the public agenda as they determine markets. If our experiment with democracy evolves into a plutocracy or *corporatocracy*—my worst world scenario—we will have only ourselves, not technology, to blame.

FROM THE FUTURE, LOOKING BACK

Today is October 1, 2008. In a little over 30 days from now will begin the first month-long voting period for a general election in the United States. The turnout is expected to top 98 percent of those citizens eligible to vote. This relatively high number of persons expected to cast votes is due to a number of significant reforms enacted by Congress following the "boycotted" election of 2004, when voter turnout reached an embarrassing low—representing a mere 22 percent of the electorate. The old saw, "What if we gave an election and no one came," was too close for comfort in 2004. But it served as a wake-up call to all the people of the United States, including the almost 80 percent of non-voters. In the next presidential election, they could either re-create civil society and exercise their potential power or simply amuse themselves to death with the large variety of electronic soma available to those connected to the wired nation.

The reasons for the especially low turnout, according to a number of respected polls (e.g., The Disney/NYT Company, Times-Warner-Westinghouse, Inc., AT&TCI/Microsoft/Sony Ltd., among others) was that American voters had somehow become disillusioned, disaffected, alienated, or just plain ambivalent about a political process and system that did not speak to them and their real needs nor represent their true interests. According to a front-page article appearing in *The Boston Globe* in mid-March of 2004, a Berlin, New Hampshire man summed up the feelings of most Americans when he said: "There is no choice. Politicians are all alike. They tell me what I want to hear, go across the street and tell you what you want to hear."[4]

The historically low turnout of 2004 was so low that the election was referred to as "The Boycotted Election of 2004." It was used to ridicule U.S. delegates at international conferences and negotiations throughout the world by several newly-wealthy but authoritarian nations of Asia, the Middle East, and South America. These nations claimed to have cultures and political systems superior to that of the United States because their citizens participated in far greater numbers in their elections. Citing the fact that elections in Taiwan in 1996 had a voter turnout of 78 percent and that turnout in the presidential election in South Africa was slightly more than 90 percent in April 1994, one foreign leader said to the American Secretary of State, "You Americans stay home amusing yourselves, having virtual experiences, and watching high-definition television."

Moreover, since the United States still had the world's highest murder rate—some 40,000 per year since repeal of all regulations against fully-automatic weapons—even iron-fisted foreign leaders would joke that the United States had the lowest voter turnout of any other democracy because: "Your people are simply afraid to go to the polls to vote for fear of being mugged or murdered." Ironically, at that time, the U.S. Department of State was still funding and otherwise supporting emerging democracies throughout the world. Apparently, American democracy was better imported than at home.

U.S. delegates and international representatives could not provide any reliable excuse to lessen their shame because the people of the nation with the longest standing democratic form of government had lost confidence in the procedures and substance of democracy to actively practice it. The term "democracy" had come to mean little more than a slogan, like "Drink Coke!" or "Just do it!" It had come to mean, for too many once hopeful people, an empty promise like "the American dream" had come to mean during the mid-to-late 20th century.

During the 10 year period from 1994–2004, the effects of globalism, privatization, deregulation, liberalization, and market reliance as the dominant arbiters of consumer welfare, coupled with the maturation of the new economy of knowledge and information, began to take their toll on traditional concepts of democracy and its institutions, "the public sphere," "civic society," and "the public interest.[5] These terms and their meanings became distorted and twisted beyond recognition. As a matter of fact, the conservative slogan that best defined this rather mean-spirited era—going back to a mid-1980s origin—was a ditty first articulated by Ronald Reagan's chairman of the Federal Communications Commission, Mark Fowler, who had said, laughingly, that "the public interest is what the public is interested in."

The FCC, under Fowler's direction and leadership, proceeded rapidly to deregulate radio and television's public trustee requirements, including their obligations to present news and informational programs, to keep and maintain programming records, or to place limits on advertising. Also, the FCC canceled broadcast stations' affirmative burden formally to ascertain the needs and interests of the communities in which they were located. Those rules had required station officials to sample public opinion from members of the general population, and, specifically, to survey community leaders. This ascertainment process provided radio and TV officials with knowledge of what was important in their local communities.

But, because of the belief that the market would satisfy consumer welfare, deregulation drove broadcast stations in the

1980s to become pure entertainment machines where even the news lost its edge because news too had to produce a profit or be cut. In order to meet its new demand, news evolved into *infotainment*. More and more, political campaigns were covered superficially as horse-races or as personality contests, rather than as debates of clearly defined issues and values that represented a choice to the viewing electorate.

Unfortunately, because of the competitive pressure of bottom-line journalism, the electorate became less and less informed. By 1987, the so-called Fairness Doctrine was eliminated. Thus, in addition to having no mandate to present any news or informational programs, radio and television stations had no obligation or inclination to present any controversial issues of public importance, nor did they explore the nuances in contrasting views on these subjects. It was no wonder that in the 1990s the public was primarily interested in diversions and amusements rather than *real* politics. Citizens were effectively offered no relevant choice, while, ironically, the number of channels multiplied and grew.

Freedom *of choice* was the American illusion; freedom *from choice* was the reality. Had real or meaningful choice been available, the general public would not have allowed its government to deteriorate as it did. By the late 1990s, it was becoming clear that there were too few alternative choices of candidates or policies competing for public acceptance. One of the chief reasons was the high cost of running for office. The barrier of money filtered out all but clones of one another, representing very similar viewpoints on issues, but with slight variations. As a consequence, good people began to lose their desire to serve or participate as citizens.

Another key reason for citizen turnoff was the widely held perception by ordinary Americans that their participation did not matter. The primary function of government appeared to be promoting the narrow interests of non-elected, non-human, non-citizen multinational corporations that too often bullied government officials at all levels by threatening that they would cut off political contributions and jobs if government attempted to burden them with the imposition of *excessive* taxes or regulations.[6] By the year 1999, almost any regulation or tax, no matter how small or necessary, began to fit the large corporations' definition of excessive. What was once understood as protecting the public interest was excoriated as heavy-handed regulatory browbeating that discouraged competition and efficiency.

As time moved on, corporations began not only to define what was or wasn't the appropriate role of government, but most of society's core values. Corporate culture became American culture and vice versa. This transformation was not difficult to understand since corporations owned the mass media; corporations controlled all channels of communicating values; corporations were setting agendas both private and public. Their core value was simple and straight to the point: Freedom to compete in local and global markets, efficiently and effectively. Democracy and free market capitalism were the same thing to the multinational corporations. To them, consumers were paramount; citizens were merely potential customers.

In the mature era of globalization, communications satellites, and the *superinformationentertainment highway*—as the privately owned, interconnected digital networks came to be called by 2001—the giant corporations were, in effect, governments unto themselves, that virtually orchestrated public opinion, public discussion, and the public agenda. Political campaigning became a mere ritual of changing personalities for an audience. Citizens were no longer invited to take a hard look at their situation. It began to seem pointless to hold government and government officials accountable for their performance in office. The people simply did not get enough relevant information to make rational choices.

Because the mass media was becoming more and more concentrated, fewer and fewer viewpoints were made available. Marginal views and dissenting opinions were dismissed from the remaining mainstream. Popular audio and video information was purposely sanitized in order to not offend potential consumers or to get them really thinking about mobilizing around political issues. Public issues that appeared on broadcast radio and television were presented in a sensational manner, but were not really of public importance if they were controversial. This was particularly the case on talk radio and daytime television infotainment programs. Thus, the political discussion that appeared on broadcasting was non-threatening to the status quo, although it was always commercial, entertaining, violent (not withstanding the V-chip), superficial, and, most of all, irrelevant to the needs of a society in transition. Political information, where serious discussion or facts appeared, was almost exclusively in text format on the pages of the few remaining newspapers that survived the bankruptcy and takeovers of the years 1999–2003. The Internet also developed into a very reliable and valuable source of political information. But by the year 2000, only 50 percent of U.S. households had access to it. "On-liners," those who could afford to connect to the *superinformationentertainment highway* and to subscribe to several of the many commercial services selling information, were rich with information. They were almost too rich, to the point of glut. Therefore, many on-liners tended to rely on digital proxies to make up their minds for them. Too little time, too much information to surf.

This, of course, created the need for the virtual political party that collected, synthesized, filtered, and transmitted politically appropriate information to Internet users who were predetermined as supporting certain issues and candidates of the virtual political party or digital lobbyist. These political information providers would scan the net to pick up pieces of useful information based on how or what information an individual or member of a household consumes. They would then develop an electronic profile based on scientific probability analysis procedures that were created to identify attitudes and predict behavior. These virtual political watch dogs then fed political information to potential voters much the way *smart agents* (discussed below) filtered and distributed information to busy executives. Attitudes and information consumption behavior of on-line users not adequately encrypted left a trail of digital "crumbs" that could be detected by digital accountants or detectives using tracer software called "cookies." Moreover, the users' trail of information consumption was in the public domain since the network is in plain view and public.

As a result of the new technology, issues and information concerning campaigns, politicians, and election results was readily available to some Americans. These Americans comprised the *information-rich* class. They had upscale incomes of more than $50,000 per year and they had higher levels of education, including a disproportionate number of college graduates and professionals. This demographic group had access to an abundance of digital information. They provided the source of revenue that enabled the information publishers and distributors to work the magic of the market, selling for a profit information that once was freely given away as public goods. Thus, they were not only the best informed members of society, they were also the most well-to-do. Of course, they were also politically powerful, using the access to information to reaffirm the status quo that allowed them to enjoy their current privilege.

"On-liners," as these digital information consumers were called, had ready access to a multitude of opinions and editorial views—but in this case many views did not mean many viewpoints. Consumer/citizen choices of entertainment and political information merely reaffirmed their preexisting prejudices, or, "sophisticated tastes," as they were conditioned to call their predilections. As a matter of fact, many digital consumers or on-liners actually subscribed to "smart agents" that had become popular during the late 1990s. Smart agents were essentially electronic versions of clipping services that individually provided a set of information tailored to meet predetermined needs and/or desires. Also available to the information-rich was data, news, chat, or whatever they wanted from a variety of free and commercial electronic newspapers, bulletin boards, web sites, or on-line chat stations, including those that provide points of view from the middle to the extremes. For those with access, the Internet had become the closest thing to the public sphere.

The Internet, however, was utilized by less than half of the American population. As a consequence, much information of critical importance never reached the plain of public debate or entered into the conversation of the masses that depended primarily on television for their information. This "information-gap" caused citizens to arrive at a different decision on candidates or issues. And the problem got worse in the year 2001, when the FCC ruled that the period of transition from the more than 50-year-old NTSC broadcast television standard would be finally phased out as obsolete and replaced by the new high-definition television (HDTV) standard.

Because of the relatively expensive cost of a new HDTV television receiver (between $1,000–$4,000 a set—not everyone could afford the new receivers, especially not low-income households disproportionally made up of African Americans, Latino Americans, single heads of households (unmarried women, and their children)—the universal access to broadcast television was lost. It became even more difficult for the common person to get current information, infotainment, or cheap entertainment. Therefore, poor people began to depend on radio as their primary source of information. They continued to use their now obsolete television sets and VCRs to watch old television programs and movies while the information-rich watched slick pay-per-view, state-of-the-art movies and sporting events, or played on-line computer games or took virtual trips in high-definition on huge vivid screens. And, since HDTV was essentially a big screen computer monitor, the Internet could be accessed and viewed clearly, remotely from anywhere in a room. As a matter of fact, "television programs" were now transmitted via the expanded, broadband, optical fiber-based Internet, as well as directly via communication satellites—all in the new high-definition, digital format. The most popular advertiser supported programs were still sitcoms, drama series, movies, and sports.

The general election of 2000 was significant due to its sameness. The election of 2000 was essentially the same as the general election of 1996, only more so: excesses of money, lobbying, and negative advertising, and the lack of genuine or serious discussion on issues, controversies, or possible solutions offered by the candidates themselves. In four years, the political sound bite had shrunk from seven seconds to five seconds of babble. And without public radio being funded earlier in that year, there was practically no meaningful public political information except to those citizens who read *The New York Times* or *The Washington Post* or those who were logged onto the Internet where rich and full conversations, dialogue, discussion, and political information services were to be found in abundance—that is, for those who knew how to search and were interested.

The only problem was that not everyone had such rich access. Only about 27 percent of U.S. households were actually using political information provided on-line, although some 50 percent of U.S. households actually had access to the emerging superinformationentertainment wire or wireless network of networks. Most Americans then, even when given the choice, selected among the 10,000 or more channels of entertainment or infotainment—from virtual experiences with dream dates to virtual competition in make-believe sporting events or astral traveling towards pseudo-knowledge; few had time to explore real politics. "It was the job of professionals to keep up with politics," said Joe Average, "I want my HDTV-MTV-Pay-Per-View-Movie. And I want it now!"

But for concerned citizens, the net provided a wealth of political information. For the political information junky there was lots of political information. But there was also much political info-junk. The really good material included on-line voter guides, modeled after projects initiated in the spring of 1996 by the California Voter Foundation,[7] and on-line disclosures of all campaign finance and lobbying expenditure information, modeled from legislation introduced by California State Assemblywoman Jackie Speier, that required all state level candidates and lobbying entities to electronically file all campaign information with the Secretary of State. The Secretary of State then made the filings immediately available on the Internet, enabling government watchdog organizations and members of the public to review current disclosures or services such as PoliticsUSA On-Line, the daily feed of political gossip and facts.

The problem with the availability of rich, textual information for some (elites) while the great majority of citizens relied on broadcast information is that the national plebiscite was ill-educated, thus favoring the elites. Research had shown that those whose primary source of news is print are able to articulate arguments for their positions on issues and choices of candidates, while those whose primary source of news is radio and television may have positions and candidates but are not able to articulate their reasoning. Perhaps this is so because those who rely on broadcasting are primarily fed empty but momentarily satisfying emotional appeals rather than substance. In any event, in the year 2000, the Fox Television Network was still the only television network to provide free air time to leading presidential candidates, including an hour on election eve. In addition to the provision of one hour on election eve to each leading presidential candidate, Fox provided a second hour of live, in-person coverage in two-minute segments during prime time, beginning 31 days prior to the election. But of Fox's more than 1,400 affiliates, more than 75 percent refused to run the segments or the one-hour election eve access program.[8]

Because so many Americans had long ago discovered how to program their V-chips to filter out 'undesirable' programs containing excessive violence and sex, early in the year 2002, a group of hackers discovered how to re-engineer the V-chip devices to filter out television commercials. By the year 2004, many television viewers were filtering out political ads as well. Although illegal, since the advertising industry successfully lobbied Congress to ban the super-V-chips that eliminated ads on the argument that they would undermine the financial base of advertiser supported 'free' television, many citizens continued to use them, especially to filter out negative political campaign ads and the mud-slinging that had become a norm of the 'good campaign'. "The super-V-chip does no less than the remote control device," claimed Congressman R. Nader of the Green Party.

The only information about the election came from campaign commercials; very few Americans watched commercial television. Those who could afford to watch could also afford the super-V-chip. They did hold an election in 2004, but no one came.

Upon analyzing the demographic makeup of those who actually voted, through exit polling techniques and electronic means, it became apparent to all that the 22 percent of the electorate who actually voted were primarily information-worker elites that represented a primary stakeholder class in support of the status quo. The election of 2004 was the first to use home-based personal computers and the superinformationentertainment highway to both register and vote.

The relatively satisfied citizen wanting to ratify and confirm that "I'm all right, Jack!" and "I've got mine, now you earn yours," comprised the group who were most likely to vote in the general election of 2004. They tended to be made up primarily of young, white, highly educated, citizens with above-average and higher incomes, who resided in a variety of places including wilderness areas and beach homes. Telecommuters, programmers, writers, smart agents, instructors, teachers, and "problem-solvers," were the job descriptions of the largest segment of voters in the election of 2004. But their skills and facility with computers and in the digital information environment did not protect them from participating in an election which later turned out to be tainted with fraud and misconduct.

The incumbent tried to steal the election by changing votes by manipulating the bits.

Several months after the incumbent administration had been sworn in and the president had given his State of the Union address, evidence began appearing that computer security was inadequate to protect the integrity of the ballots. Rogue security agents within government had tampered with the National Vote-Counter Computer System by placing a stealth virus into the tabulation software to enable a change in every 100th vote for the opposition candidate into a vote for the incumbent in those states where the race was close.

Moreover, it is now believed that the incumbent administration may have used new second generation "clipper chip" technology to identify individual voter ballots and to create huge enemies lists, next to which the attempt to identify political opponents during the Nixon administration pales. The case is still being investigated by the Office of the Special Prosecutor.

It now appears certain that electronic ballots were not secret ballots at all. Anyone who voted with their computer did so openly. It was subsequently pointed out that any technology that can continuously verify the identity of computer users inherently can violate voter privacy and security. "But without such verification technology," the incumbent administration argued, "ineligible persons such as non-citizens, children, felons, and the insane would vote illegally."

"Security is an illusion!," shouted Opra D. Gates, an official with the *NII Liberation Front.* "No computer network is absolutely secure from us. We can break into any data bank in the world if given enough time." (The NII Liberation Front is a hacker group that, in 2002, penetrated secure commercial systems and even the

U.S. Department of Defense firewall-protected systems, using "snifter" software to gain illegal access.

Civil rights groups had made another set of arguments against computer voting that merited consideration on equity grounds. They said: "Since only 60 percent of U.S. households had access to either a personal computer or a network computer, the concept of one-person, one-vote had been undermined." Poor people generally, racial minorities, and even the elderly, were disproportionately without access to the means of voting electronically—so they stayed home, particularly during the record-setting cold weather in the Northeast and Midwestern parts of the nation during the month of November. And, because of the relatively high cost of going on-line, the new computer balloting was tantamount to a new form of poll-tax. In addition, due to the broader and deeper levels of literacy required to use complex computers and software, electronic voting represented a literacy test that kept almost one-third of the adult population at home on election day.

When the numbers came in reporting on the unprecedented low voter turnout, not only were the candidates dumbfounded, even citizens who failed to exercise their franchise by their failure to vote "because it wouldn't make a difference anyway" realized that something had radically and profoundly changed our political culture. Everyone was frightened that the government elected into power had very little legitimacy and practically no mandate to represent the collective will of the people.

The president was elected by only 14.5 percent of all eligible voters. Up to this point, no one really took the responsibility of civil society seriously nor was there any meaningful attempt toward significant political reform. Ironically, anyone who even suggested dramatic but necessary reform previously was labeled such divisive terms as "anti-democratic," "left-wing," and/or "radical rabble-rousers." Incumbent politicians, lobbyists as well as the eight colossal, conglomerate media and communications firms that dominated access and the flow of culture were quite satisfied with the status quo until the surprising election of 2004. To them, prior to the election of 2004, America had the best political system in the world. The old system of politics had been theirs for the buying.

As a result of the disastrous presidential election of 2004, peoples' viewing and information consumption habits began to change. The burning issues following the election of 2004 were American democracy and its possible demise, or as some cynics said, its evolution into "corporate plutocracy." Ironically, radical solutions offered by marginalized groups ultimately provided the ideas essential to save the Republic.

"Democracy Now" movements sprung up spontaneously across the United States. They began to sweep the nation. Chants from the 1960s were heard from city to city: "Power to the People! More Power to the People!"

Citizens began to demonstrate at public places, claiming them as "demospheres"—places where citizens addressed government openly in rational and public deliberations about what kind of society they wanted and what actions of government would be necessary to promote the common good. These public rallies were not dissimilar to those that occurred at Tienanmen Square in China during the early 1990s, but without, of course, the state or corporate security forces using tanks or authoritarian suppression techniques against the citizens (probably because the public and private police were, in the final analysis, also angry citizens). The American people just could not take being treated as mere consumers any longer. They demanded to be treated with the respect accorded citizens.

By the year 2005, the people demanded full citizenship and assumed their responsibility to act accordingly, towards building a better civic society. No more could the American people stand by or sit idly watching HDTV while their democracy was being advertised, sold, lobbied, and traded away like pork bellies, electronic digits, or widgets in the marketplace. The poor showing of American democracy in the Boycotted Election of 2004 was a wake-up call for the average citizen to create a true government by The People, for The People, and of The People.

No one seemed to be paying attention to the electorate. Because the previous voter turnout for the election of 2000 was down to only 33 percent of those eligible, continuing a decades-long slide, no one worried at the time, except a few scholars and marginalized groups who didn't own or watch HDTV. Politicians, candidates, spin doctors, and television executives all had been taking citizens and the interests of citizens for granted and, as a consequence, they were all blind-sided by the results of the Boycotted Election of 2004. And by what it represented—a vote of no confidence in what then remained of American democratic institutions, a national mirage with little substance.

"What Kind Of Society Have We Become?" "Where Do We Go From Here?" "Don't We Care Anymore About Our National Interests?" "It's Wake Up Time—Democracy On The Brink" were the headlines on the day after the 2004 election in the four remaining hard-text national newspapers.

Now, almost four years later, just a month prior to the next general election, knowledgeable sources are predicting a historically high voter turnout. Almost 99 percent of those citizens eligible to vote are expected to actually turn out and vote.

During the month-long period,[9] in which some 180 million registered adult citizens will go into a voting booth or mail in their ballots, there will be public ceremonies, teach-ins, and real affirmative participation by people at public places in their communities. These efforts are aimed towards building democratic bridges of and including all the people not just politically, but also civically and socially in American society and culture.

The primary reason for such jubilant celebration concerning the ensuing election is perhaps provided in large measure by the market incentive to vote—*The Lottery*—that is being called "The Great American Dream Machine" which lubricates democracy in the United States. But, first, more context:

In the year 2005, Congress enacted the *Compulsory Voter Registration Act* that requires the 50 states as well as the District of Columbia and U.S. Territories to register all U.S. citizens 18 years of age or older that are, or would be 18 years old any time prior to midnight on the last day of the month-long voting period.

Because the federal government under the new law has authority to withhold a percentage of money from federal block grants to the states, equal to twice the percentage of unregistered voters in a state, states have ample incentive to enforce the voter registration. Consequently, the various states have enacted local mandatory registration laws and a system of monetary fines that start at $10 during the first three-month period after a minor turns 18. Thereafter, the state may fine an individual for failing to register to vote in amounts that increase by $10 per month for each month he is not registered, until the total of the fine reaches $250. While all citizens have an affirmative duty to register to vote, there is no legal requirement that they actually vote. Instead, affirmative incentives are provided for that.

Registration is now very easy. A person may register by mail, at public schools, at post offices, on their jobs, at their cable/telephone/TV utility company when paying their monthly information bill, or at any government agency. The information utility companies automatically provide notices to people within 60 days prior to their 18th birthday, as a public service.

State governments are delighted with the imposition of mandatory voter registration because of the benefits they receive, including full payment of their block grant allocation, a substantial increase in the diversity on jury pools, and more accurate census counts the yield a fairer distribution of public benefits.

Privacy violation has not been a serious issue; no one worries since they are now protected by the recently ratified Constitutional Amendment guaranteeing to individuals a right to a reasonable expectation of privacy.[10] As a consequence of the new privacy amendment, Congress also enacted *The Privacy Act of 2005* that established a Federal Privacy Commission, modeled after a similar agency in Canada. In addition, the Privacy Act requires that any non-profit or commercial entity that uses an individual's name and/ or personal identifying information for any fund-raising or commercial purpose on a mailing list, print or electronic, must notify that individual, in writing, by April 15 of each year. Also, if commercial gain or profit results from the sale, lease, or rental of any such mailing list, then the business enterprise shall pay to the individual whose name or personal identifying information is used an amount totaling one-tenth of one cent per use of the name as a user fee. This legislation establishes a property ownership right in an individual's name, rewards the person for any appropriation of his name and identifying information, and guarantees notification to the individual each year so that the person whose name is being used has adequate notice of who is using his name and for what purpose (e.g., to solicit contributions, to recruit to a cause, to profit on the sale of behavioral profiles, etc.).

Responding to the wake-up call of the 2004 election, Congress came to realize that the federal government was democratic in form but not in substance. Drastic measures were now necessary to save the substance of American democracy. Therefore, both the campaign finance system and the "winner take all" plurality system had to be changed radically. Money and the unfairness of the "first past the post" plurality system, that encourages a two-party monopoly (because votes for third parties are wasted) and rewards the gerrymandering of single-member districts to give parties or particular racial groups built-in advantages, had to be taken out of politics.[11]

First, regarding the undue influence of money, the easy solution offered by Congressional moderates was merely to prohibit any paid advertising on broadcast radio and television. But, because more and more viewers of television were filtering out political ads with their super-V-chips, fewer potential voters were watching political advertisements anyway. Moreover, by this time, most political campaign money was being spent on reaching smaller, discrete, targeted audiences through the new technologies, primarily the Internet that now transmitted television programs, movies on-demand, and cable fare.[12] Therefore, something radical was required to minimize the influence of money on political campaigns. The solution ultimately reached by Congress was to ban all political advertising and to require both print and electronic media to provide free public service notices.[13]

Next, Congress showed even more leadership and courage by eliminating the plurality system and replacing it with a "party-list system" of *proportional representation*.[14] Now, the states are divided into multimember districts, where several political parties present lists of candidates within each multimember district. The voter selects one party and its slate of candidates to represent him. Party slates can be either "closed or "open," allowing voters to indicate a preference for individual candidates. If a party receives 30 percent of the seats in the legislature, 10 percent of the vote receives 10 percent of the seats, and so on.

This new proportional representation system encourages multiparty democracy because it permits even small parties to elect representatives. Environmentalists, labor, and consumer parties are now among the interests being represented in the new Congress. In order to qualify as a viable political party under this new system, parties must pass a minimum threshold of the total vote; extremist parties have been checked by a 5 percent threshold. One of the key benefits of the new proportional representation system is that it has reduced the incentives to engage in partisan or racial gerrymandering because every significant party or voting bloc in the multimember districts is represented more or less in proportion to its strength in the entire electorate, regardless of how the district lines were drawn. Moreover, this new system is encouraging greater citizen participation in government because everyone now feels that his interests are being represented and his vote now makes a difference.

Other significant political reforms that promote the "New Democracy Movement" include provisions of the *Universal Service and Access to Information and Technology Act of 2005*.[15] This law defines "Universal Service and Access" as requiring "for all the people of the United States," accessibility to 1) essential information; 2) appropriate information technology; 3) audiences, both small (one-to-one) and mass (broadcasting); 4) the means (funding) for producing information in digital formats and distributing them; and 5) a reasonable right of privacy.[16]

The privacy provisions of the Act became law prior to the ratification of the new Constitutional amendment, but were necessary at the time because too many users of on-line communications services were reluctant to provide personal or financial data. Users' concerns stemmed from the high possibility of fraud or privacy abuse, notwithstanding the pleas of digital entrepreneurs who said, "It's safe. Trust me."

"Essential information" has been interpreted to mean, among other things, public information that government keeps, maintains, processes, and uses in the course of doing government work; that information which taxpayers have paid for—with the exception of government information that was subject to exceptions under the Freedom of Information Act (FOIA). Thus, information concerning criminal investigations, personnel records, national defense and security, etc., are still not available to the general public. Moreover, access to the Internet and e-mail[17] have now been deemed as essential information services, as well as public education—from cradle to grave, if an individual wants to take advantage of this public utility. Public broadcasting and video are also essential under the Act.

"Appropriate information technology" has been defined to mean a wide range of digital technology, delivered via radio and by wire, as well as the hardware for receiving digital signals from wireless and wired services. This provision was found to be necessary in order to create a truly *national* National Information Infrastructure. The hands-off approach of market reliance had led to a form of digital feudalism.

Although the mega-huge telecommunications companies had at one time competed vigorously with one another, by the year 2001 it was obvious that "market competition" was a concept of a different age—as reflected by the lack of any significant antitrust enforcement in decades. This was the case even though the Baby Bells, cable companies and former long distance service providers (AT&T, MCI, and Sprint) had merged with one another or entered into some form of strategic alliance in order to compete globally.

The threat of global competition seemed to have made real competition in the domestic market unnecessary and undesirable. Bigness was now thought to be necessary in order to give "American Champions" playing in the global arena a competitive edge against foreign-based multinational corporations. It was a sort of economic nationalism that seem to regard corporations as super citizens. But these giant media-information-entertainment-communications corporations did not necessarily promote the interests of Americans, at least not those who were not stockholders. Because large segments of society simply could not afford access to the conglomerates' services, they were passed over as the "undeserving poor." Thus, the gap between the rich and poor grew wider—that is, until Congress passed the historic *Information Access Act of 2005,* in order "to unite the peoples of America with a common public information infrastructure and to promote the national defense." Accordingly, access to both the common carrier Public Broadcast Network and access to the National Public Telecommunication Network was mandated.

With these new network services, government has again become the service provider of last resort by developing and making available appropriate information technology and software enabling all the people of the United States to be productive, creative, and self-realized members of a national community.

Funding for the development of the public infrastructure and public information products and services (on both the public wire[18] and public air) is obtained by charging all commercial users of public airwaves reasonable user fees. This continuous revenue source would not have been available had Congress allowed the sale of broadcast frequencies during the late-1990s as certain special interests had lobbied for.[19] This arrangement was thought to be only fair since the $100 billion investment that the public had made in the old, now obsolete NTSC television technology was lost. There is also a 10 percent surcharge on the purchase of new digital TV sets. Since over the air television reception is now restricted to the new HDTV or Advanced TV standards that are incompatible with the now obsolete NTSC standard, enough surplus revenue has been collected to build an endowment for a Public Information Trust that distributes funding grants and subsidies to independent makers of public information products, goods, and services in various formats.

Wire-delivered services on the public broadband fiber network include e-mail service that greatly relieves the old U.S. Postal Service. The broadband optical network provides all the people of the United States with efficient access to essential public information, including public education, civic information, medical and health care information, and information regarding any government function or service. As a matter of fact, all government records and public information that were not otherwise legally classified under exceptions to the Freedom of Information Act are now available on public networks.

This public information utility was justified on the basis of enhancing America's national defense—in accord with the long standing mandate of Title I, Section 1 of *The Communications Act of 1934, as amended.* The underlying rationale is that the real threat to our national security, and what is needed to safeguard our defense in the long run, are a strong and viable workforce—one that is intelligent and educated—and an inclusive, cohesive society capable of winning global competition in knowledge markets. The national defense rationale, after all, provided government incentives in education and training after the Soviet Union successfully launched the world's first man-made communications satellite, Sputnik. Our response was to invest in educating our children and adult populations. Education and information was then deemed to be a strategic resource and a weapon against ignorance and tyranny. In response to Sputnik, the Eisenhower administration launched the National Defense Education Act. Now, in our present global crisis following the near-collapse of American democracy, a similarly appropriate response was called for and adopted.

On the broadcast end, due to the recognition that digital compression technology could multiply the number of television channels by four-fold or ten-fold, scarcity was no longer a restraining barrier that ought to keep the airwaves out of the hands of the people. Therefore, Congress enacted laws that set aside, in each market, six terrestrial broadcast channels and six direct satellite broadcast channels as a dedicated public network of common carrier channels. The satellite broadcast channels provide nation-wide and regional programming services that include independent non-profit television programming, a C-SPAN-type service with regional, state-wide, and national government programming, a public education/literacy network, a children's television network, and a First Amendment-Free Speech-Demosphere channel, where political issues are debated and discussed and where candidates for national and state-wide office have free but limited access. The same types of services are available for earth-based television channels set aside for these purposes. Also, no radio or television station, or any media entity, may sell political advertisements. Such advertisements are banned, although any broadcast radio or television station may offer any amount of free time to any candidate for public office, so long as all other legally qualified candidates for the same office are offered an equal opportunity of access.

Public schools are now required to teach a new media literacy curriculum, consisting of a range of courses that attempt to empower individuals with critical thinking and communication skills, as well as a core body of information concerning democracy, civil culture, and civics. The intent of these courses is to teach all the people of the United States how to survive and succeed in the information-knowledge-global economy. For example, beginning as early as the kindergarten, children would be taught not only traditional literacy skills, but also how to listen critically and how to communicate effectively; how to recognize propaganda and to deconstruct messages of all sorts, including messages of the media; how to analyze cartoons, commercials, movies, books, and news-papers; and, as they advance in age, how to effectively use information technologies such as computers, digital recording, display devices, etc., and how to create their own messages, writings, graphics, videos, art, music, etc. On-line and broadcast education is also available 24 hours a day to supplement in-class teaching. Equal educational opportunities are provided to all of the people of the United States, from cradle to grave. Life-long learning is no longer the exception, but the norm. The national objective of public education, besides skills acquisition, is to develop an objectively informed and intellectually vigorous citizenry—an informed and active public.

CONCLUSION

In conclusion, a few words on the prime reason for the expected record-high voter turnout for the election of 2008. It is indeed *The Lottery,* touted as "The Great American Dream Ballot Box." In each state or territory during a presidential election, the federal government would contribute 25 cents per voter into a state voter lottery. A single voter in each state would win the lottery, notwithstanding who they voted for, so long as they voted during the month-long period that the polls would remain open. A lottery of this sort would get almost everyone eligible to the voting booth for the chance of realizing two American dreams—the chance of becoming instantly wealthy and the opportunity to exercise a meaningful vote.

When I explained this lottery scheme to one of my colleagues at Harvard, as a means of maximizing voter turnout, I was presented with the following reply: "But who would want all those people to vote anyway?"

I thought about this response a lot since then—"Who would want *all those people* to vote anyway?"

That response reveals the real problem with contemporary elections, campaigning, and voting in the United States. The problem is not technology, per se. It is power, *per se*. Comfortable elites simply don't want others included in the equation of American democracy, regardless of what technology is available or utilized. Until we rethink that equation, democracy remains an illusion. In the present equation, elections are won by minimizing choice and the opportunity for people to make real decisions. Yet, elections should be, and in the year 2008, they may finally be about maximizing real choice and the opportunity of ordinary citizens to participate in making those choices—by whatever technology necessary.

ENDNOTES

1. "... [T]he transformation of the information infrastructure and emergence of the "net"—the telecommunications network—as the dominant medium has led to a wide variety of frustrations for nation-states as they attempt to exercise traditional modes of power, such as control over either financial or information flows across their borders . . . transnational corporations have come to rival and sometimes outweigh nation-states in the exercise of a variety of forms of power. . . ." William Berry, et al., *Last Rights: Revisiting Four Theories of the Press,* ed. John C. Nerone (Urbana, IL: University of Illinois Press, 1995), p. 160.

2. Here, I assume that the more things change, the more they will stay the same, or as Dwight D. Eisenhower is quoted as having said: "Things are more like they are today than they have ever been before." Jack Dann and Gardner Dozois, ed., *Future Power: A Science Fiction Anthology* (New York: Random House, 1976).

3. More appropriately called the "demosphere," according to Ronnie Dugger, publisher of *The Texas Observer* and Fellow of the Shorenstein Center on the Press, Politics and Public Policy, Kennedy School of Government, Harvard University, spring term, 1996.

4. Actual quotation of Lion Caron of Berlin, NH, *The Boston Globe,* March 22, 1996, p. 1.

5. McWorld" [globalism and universal markets] makes "national borders porous from without." Like the Jihad, "McWorld . . . make[s] war on the sovereign

nation-state and thus undermine[s] the nation-state's democratic institutions . . . [It] eschews civil society and belittles democratic citizenship, . . . indifferen[t] to civil liberty. Jihad forges communities of blood rooted in exclusion and hatred, communities that slight democracy in favor of tyrannical paternalism or consensual tribalism. McWorld forges global markets rooted in consumption and profit, leaving to an untrustworthy, if not altogether fictitious invisible hand issues of public interest and common good that once might have been nurtured, by democratic citizenries and their watchful governments. . . ." Benjamin R. Barber, *Jihad vs. McWorld* (New York: Times Books/Random House, 1995), pp. 6–7.

6. Pollster Daniel Yankelovich rebuts the conventional wisdom that the decline in participation by Americans in presidential and congressional elections is due to voter apathy—the view that Americans do not get involved because they do not care. Instead, he claims that, "The chief reason so many Americans do not vote is because they do not think their votes will make a difference." He goes on to say, "Beneath the surface of formal arrangements to ensure citizen participation, the political reality is that an intangible something [a barrier] separates the general public from the thin layer of elites—officials, experts, and leaders who hold the real power and make the important decisions." That barrier that exists between America's elites and its average citizens is, according to Yankelovich, intellectual snobbery. Whereupon he offers the following observation:

"An adversarial struggle exists between experts and the public on who will govern America. On one side are the experts—smaller in number and weaker than the public in formal power but holding an indispensable piece of the solution. As a group, these experts respect the institution of democracy and would be chagrined if their good faith were challenged. At the same time, however, their view of the general public is that it is ill-informed and ill-equipped to deal with the problems to which they, the experts, have devoted their lives. . . .

"Unfortunately, . . . most average citizens are ill-prepared to exercise their responsibilities for self-governance, even though they have a deep-seated desire to have more of a say in decisions. People want their opinions heeded—not every whim and impulse that may be registered in an opinion poll, but their thoughtful, considered judgments. But in present-day America, few institutions are devoted to helping the public to form considered judgments, and the public is discouraged from doing the necessary hard work because there is little incentive to do so. In principle, the people are sovereign. In practice, the experts and technocrats have spilled over their legitimate boundaries and are encroaching on the public's territory." Daniel Yankelovich, *Coming To Public Judgment: Making Democracy Work in a Complex World* (Syracuse, NY: Syracuse University Press, 1991), pp. 3–4.

7. The California Voter Foundation is a non-partisan, non-profit organization based in Sacramento. The 1996 voter guide was produced in partnership with California Secretary of State Bill Jones, who also unveiled two new web sites: the 1996 California Primary Election Server, which features live returns on election night (http://www.primary96.ca.gov) and the California Secretary of

State Home Page (http://www.primary96.ss.ca.gov). Voters can use the 1996 California Online Voter Guide to find information about statewide ballot measures as well as presidential, congressional, legislative, and local candidates running in California.

In 1994, CVF produced its first on-line guide, which was accessed 14,000 times and registered over 36,000 file retrievals. In 1995, CVF produced the San Francisco Online Voter Guide, which featured the first Internet database of campaign contributions and expenditures. The San Francisco guide registered over 23,000 file retrievals prior to the election, and was rated by *PC Magazine* as one of the top 100 web sites of 1995. For more information, contact Kim Alexander, Executive Director, California Voter Foundation, (916-325-2120, e-mail: <kimalex@netcom.com>, website: http://www.webcom.com/cvf/).

8. By 1997, the Federal Communications Commission had established a HDTV standard, but instead of making it the standard mandatory, it allowed TV broadcasters the discretion to adopt HDTV or split their 6MHz frequency into four, six, eight or even sixteen digital Advanced TV channels, which most of the industry did in order to increase their revenue streams. The irony of this abundance of television channels was that programming was just as bad and non-innovative; and, moreover, only a handful of TV licensees saw themselves as public trustees, except in name only. Neither the HDTV or the Advanced TV standards were compatible with NTSC, however.

9. According to John Deardourff of The Media Company, one of the country's leading political strategists and a pioneer of political advertising, the citizens of the State of Texas may already vote up to 20 days leading to the close of certain state and local elections. Statement made during a "Brown Bag Lunch" at the Shorenstein Center on the Press, Politics and Public Policy, Kennedy School of Government, Harvard University, April 15, 1996.

10. Such an Amendment could be modeled after the provision in the Constitution of the Republic of South Africa, ACT NO. 200, 1993, under Chapter 3, 13, which states: "Every person shall have the right to his or her personal privacy, which shall include the right not to be the subject to searches of his or her person, home, or property, the seizure of private possessions *or the violation of private communications.*"(Emphasis added). Note: The State of California also has an amendment in its constitution guaranteeing a right to privacy.

11. Michael Lind, "Prescription for a New National Democracy," *Political Science Quarterly,* 110, No. 4, 1995–96, pp. 563–86.

12. ". . . [D]espite their limitations, new media are replacing the press as conduits for information flows from governments to people and from people to governments. In similar fashion, the press is losing its privileged role as a definer of facticity." Neron, Id., *Last Rights,* p.174. Also, trends in media technology are towards replacing broad audiences with increasingly narrow ones.

13. "Candidates without enormous amounts of money, either from their own fortunes or from rich individuals and special interest groups, cannot hope to win party primaries, much less general elections. Indeed, the *Buckley* decision is one reason why more than half of the members of the Senate today are millionaires [citation omitted]. The bias toward the rich embodied in

American campaign finance practices makes a mockery of America's democratic ideals. Genuine democracy requires not only juridical equality among races when it comes to individual rights, but also political equality among the different socioeconomic classes of citizens.

"It is time to build a wall of separation between check and state. Curing the disease of plutocratic politics requires a correct diagnosis of its cause: the costs of political advertising. The basic problem is that special interests buy access and favors by donating the money needed for expensive political advertising in the media. Elaborate schemes governing the flow of money do nothing to address the central problem: paid political advertising. Instead of devising unworkable limits on campaign financing that leave the basic system intact, we should cut the Gordian knot of campaign corruption by simply outlawing paid political advertising on behalf of any candidate for public office. The replacement of political advertising by free informational public service notices in the electronic and print media would level the playing field of politics and kill off an entire parasitic industry of media consultants and spin doctors.

"An outright ban on paid political advertising and the imposition of free time requirements on the media are radical measures, but nothing less is necessary if we are to prevent our government from continuing to be sold to the highest bidders. The argument against strict public regulation of money in politics is based on a false analogy between free spending and free speech protected under the First Amendment. The analogy is false, because limits on campaign finance do not address the content of speech—only its volume, as it were. It is not an infringement on free speech to say that, in a large public auditorium, Douglas will not be allowed to use a microphone unless Lincoln can as well." Michael Lind, "Prescriptions for a New National Democracy," *Political Science Quarterly,* 110, No. 4, 1995–96, p.570.

14. There are many different types of proportional representation (PR). PR is the voting system used by most of the world's major democracies, because it is a flexible system that may be adapted to the situation of any city, state, or nation. Besides the list system, mentioned above, three additional types most commonly used are: 1) Mixed Member System. This PR hybrid elects half the legislature from single-seat, "winner take all" districts and the other half by the List System. The Mixed Member System smoothly combines geographic, ideological, and proportional representation; 2) Preference Voting (PV). The voter simply ranks candidates in an order of preference (1, 2, 3, 4, etc. . . .). Once a voter's first choice is elected or eliminated, excess votes are "transferred" to subsequent preferences until all positions are filled. Voters can vote for their favorite candidate(s), knowing that if that candidate doesn't receive enough votes their vote will "transfer" to their next preference. With PV, every vote counts and very few votes are wasted. PV is ideal for non-partisan elections like city councils; and 3) Majority Preference Voting (MPV). Related to PV, MPV is ideal when selecting a single candidate such as president, mayor, or governor who must win a majority. Like PV, the voter simply ranks candidates in an order of preference (i.e., 1. Clinton, 2. Dole, 3. Perot). The candidate with the least number of first place votes is

eliminated, and their votes are "transferred" to their 2nd choice until a candidate has a majority. Source: "Proportional Representation: What's it all about?" Center for Voting and Democracy, Washington, D.C. (e-mail: <cvdusa@aol.com>, website: http://www.igc.apc.org/cvd).

15. "Federal support for a national information infrastructure—a postal system— is generally justified by the need to ensure that representatives of the people can communicate with their constituents in a two-way process." Nerone, Id., p. 171. See, also: Robert H. Anderson, et al., *Universal Access To Email: Feasibility and Societal Implications* (Santa Monica, CA: RAND, 1995). Although the United States is the only nation with a "First Amendment," it is by no means the only nation that guarantees the freedoms of speech and of the press in its constitution. As a matter of fact, some nations go further by providing the guarantees to freedoms of expression and even access to information. For example, Article 21 of the Japanese Constitution, which was written by American officials within a four day time span, reads as follows:

"Freedom of assembly and association as well as speech, press, and all other forms of expression are guaranteed. No censorship shall be maintained, nor shall the secrecy of any means of communications be violated."

Moreover, the Constitution of the Republic of South Africa provides even broader freedoms. The following articles under the heading "Fundamental Rights" in Chapter 3 of the South African Constitution are examples:

"Religion, belief and opinion: 14.(1) Every person shall have the rights to freedom of conscience, religion, thought, belief, and opinion, which shall include academic freedom in institutions of higher learning. . . .

"Freedom of expression: 15.(1) Every person shall have the rights to freedom of speech and expression, which shall include freedom of the press and other media, and the freedom of artistic creativity and scientific research. (2) All media financed by or under the control of the state shall be regulated in a manner which ensures impartiality and the expression of a diversity of opinion. . . .

"Political rights: 21 (1) Every person shall have the right—(a) to form, to participate in the activities of and to recruit members for a political party; (b) to campaign for a political party or cause; and (c) to make political choices. (2) Every citizen shall have the right to vote, to do so in secret and to stand for election to public office. . . .

"Access to information: 23. Every person shall have the right of access to all information held by the state or any of its organs at any level of government in so far as such information is required for the exercise or protection of any of his or her rights. . . .

"Language and culture: 31. Every person shall have the right to use the language and to participate in the cultural life of his or her choice.

"Education: 32. Every person shall have the right—(a) to basic education and to equal access to educational institutions; (b) to instruction in the language of his or her choice where this is reasonably practicable; and (c) to establish, where practicable, educational institutions based on a common culture, language or religion, provided that there shall be no discrimination on the ground of race."

16. See, generally: Nolan Bowie, "Equity and Access to Information Technology," *The Annual Review* (Institute for Information Studies, 1990); Jorge Reina Schement and Terry Curtis, "Distributional Justice," in *Tendencies and Tensions of the Information Age* (New Brunswick: Transaction Publishers, 1995); Francis Dummer Fisher, "Open Sesame! How to Get to the Treasure of Electronic Information," in U.S. Department of Commerce, *20/20 Vision: The Development of a National Information Infrastructure*, 1994; and, Susan G. Hadden, "Universal Service: Policy Options for the Future," Benton Foundation Policy Working Paper, 1994.

17. "We find that use of electronic mail is valuable for individuals and communities, for the practice and spread of democracy, and for the general development of a viable National Information Infrastructure (NII). Consequently, the nation should support universal access to e-mail through appropriate public and private policies. . . .

"Individuals' accessibility to e-mail is hampered by increasing income, education, and racial gaps in the availability of computers and access to network services. Some policy remedies appear to be required. . . .

"It is critical that electronic mail be a basic service in a National Information Infrastructure. . . .

"It is important to reduce the increasing gaps in access to basic electronic information system services, specifically, access to electronic mail services." Anderson, et al., Id., pp. xiv–xv.

18. The public wire had its origins in the now obsolete, twisted pair telephone system used by the federal government as the emergency back-up communications service called, "FTS-2000." This system was upgraded into a national grid, based on broadband, interactive, optical fiber technology. It now provides information services to people who cannot afford commercial on-line information services as a matter of right, including the provision of e-mail and other essential information and services that the unregulated market had denied the former "information have-nots."

19. Because spectrum user fees could be collected only if the public still owned the airwaves, Congress had decided, after much debate, that it was in the public's long-term interest not to sell, via auction or otherwise, any additional radiomagnetic spectrum other than the limited amounts of microwave frequencies that had been sold during the mid-1990s for the development of personal digital services and cellular services.

Conference Participants

Jeffrey Abramson
Department of Politics
Brandeis University

Jan Witold Baran
Chairman
ABA Advisory Commission to
    the Standing Committee on
    Election Law;
Wiley, Rein & Fleming

Nolan A. Bowie
Associate Professor
Department of Broadcasting,
    Telecommunications, and
    Mass Media
Temple University

Roman Buhler
Counsel for the Committee on
    House Oversight
U.S. House of Representatives

William Canfield III
Holland & Knight

Catherine Clark
Program Manager
The John and Mary R. Markle
    Foundation

Anthony Corrado
Department of Government
Colby College

John Jay Douglass
University of Houston Law
    Center

Lee Ann Elliott
Commissioner
Federal Election Commission

Adelaide Elm
Director of Public Information
Project Vote Smart

Charles M. Firestone
Director
Communications and Society
    Program
The Aspen Institute

Frank Havlicek
Vice President
The Washington Post

Sonia R. Jarvis
National Center for Communi-
    cations Studies
George Washington University

David R. Johnson
Chairman
Counsel Connect;
Founder
Cyberspace Law Institute

Milton Morris
Vice President
Joint Center for Political and
  Economic Studies

R. Clayton Mulford
Hughes & Luce, L.L.P

Daniel R. Ortiz
School of Law
University of Virginia

Trevor Potter
Wiley, Rein & Fielding

Pauline A. Schneider
Chair
ABA Standing Committee on
  Election Law;
Hunton & Williams

Janet Studley
Holland & Knight

Scott Thomas
Commissioner
Federal Election Commission

Frank L. Tobe
Below, Tobe & Associates, Inc.

Steven Uhlfelder
Holland & Knight

Armando Valdez
President
Valdez and Associates

Christine Varney
Commissioner
Federal Trade Commission

Tracy Westen
President
Center for Governmental Studies

Observer:

Nina Houghton
Vice Chair, Program Committee
The Aspen Institute Board of
  Trustees

Staff:

Amy Korzick Garmer
Senior Program Associate
Communications and Society
  Program
The Aspen Institute

Elizabeth Yang
Staff Director
Standing Committee on Election
  Law
American Bar Association

Gia Nolan
Program Coordinator
Communications and Society
  Program
The Aspen Institute

About the Authors

Anthony Corrado is Associate Professor of Government at Colby College in Waterville, Maine, where he teaches courses on American politics and political theory. A leading expert on campaign finance and presidential elections, Corrado is currently a member of the American Bar Association's Advisory Commission on Election Law and has previously served as executive director of the Twentieth Century Fund's Task Force on Presidential Debates. His books include *Paying for Presidents* and *Creative Campaigning*. In addition to his academic work, he has been a consultant to campaigns in both the United States and Canada, and was a member of the White House staff during the Carter Administration.

Sonia R. Jarvis is Research Professor at the George Washington University, National Center for Communication Studies, in Washington, D.C. Her background includes extensive experience in grass roots community organizing, civil rights advocacy and litigation, media and public policy analysis, and communications theory. Jarvis has held visiting appointments at the Harvard University Kennedy School of Government and Georgetown University Law Center, and from 1987–1994 served as Executive Director of the National Coalition of Black Voter Participation.

Jeffrey Abramson holds the Louis Stulberg Chair in Law and Politics at Brandeis University in Waltham, Massachusetts, where he teaches law and political thought. He has written widely on law, the media, and political theory. Abramson's recent books, *We, The Jury: The Jury System and the Ideal of Democracy* and *The Electronic Commonwealth: The Impact of New Media Technologies on Democratic Politics*, have received widespread acclaim.

Tracy Westen is President of *The Democracy Network*, founder and former vice chairman of *The California Channel*, a public affairs cable television network serving the state of California, and founder and President of the Los Angeles-based Center for Governmental Studies, a nonprofit organization which seeks to improve the processes of democratic self-government in California. A former commissioner on the Board of Telecommunication Commissioners for the City of Los Angeles, Westen also teaches communications law as a Lecturer at the UCLA Law School and an Adjunct Professor at the USC-Annenberg School for Communication in Los Angeles.

Nolan A. Bowie is Associate Professor at Temple University's School of Communications and Theater, where he teaches in the Department of Broadcasting, Telecommunications and Mass Media. During the 1995–96 academic year, Bowie was Visiting Senior Fellow at The Joan Shorenstein Center on the Press, Politics and Public Policy and Visiting Lecturer in Public Policy at the John F. Kennedy School of Government, Harvard University. His primary policy concerns are with issues of equity and access to information and information technology in promoting the public's interest. In addition to his academic work, Bowie is a communications attorney with extensive professional and volunteer advocacy experience.

The Aspen Institute
Communications and Society Program

The overall goal of the Communications and Society Program is to promote integrated, thoughtful, value-based decision making in the communications and information policy fields. In particular, the Program focuses on the implications of communications and information technologies on democratic institutions, individual behavior, instruments of commerce, and community life.

The Program accomplishes this through two main types of activities. First, it brings together representatives of industry, government, the media, the academic world, the nonprofit sector, and others for roundtable meetings to assess the impact of modern communications and information systems on the ideas and practices of a democratic society. Second, the Program promotes research and distributes conference reports to leaders in the communications and information fields, and to the public at large.

Topic areas of the Program fall into three categories: the societal impact of the communications and information infrastructures, communications policy making, and communications for global understanding. Within these areas, the Program has chosen to focus with special interest on the issues of telecommunications and education, electronic democracy, media impact, and electronic commerce.

Charles Firestone is Director of The Aspen Institute's Communications and Society Program. Prior to joining the Institute, he was a private communications and entertainment attorney in Los Angeles and an adjunct professor at the UCLA School of Law, where he also directed the Communications Law Program. Firestone worked previously as an attorney at the Federal Communications Commission and as director of litigation for the Citizens Communication Center in Washington, D.C.

The American Bar Association Standing Committee on Election Law

The Standing Committee on Election Law of the American Bar Association was created in 1973 to examine and develop ways to improve the federal election process. The seven-member committee is appointed by the President of the ABA for three-year terms. The Standing Committee is aided in its activities by a ten-member Advisory Commission, which was created in 1979 to provide expertise and guidance to the committee. The commission is comprised of representatives from Congress, a representative of the League of Women Voters, the Chair and Vice Chair of the Federal Election Commission, election law attorneys, and academics.

Since its creation, the Standing Committee has studied and referred to the ABA House of Delegates numerous recommendations that have been adopted as Association policy, including but not limited to: the election of the President and Vice President by direct popular vote, support for enactment of federal legislation facilitating voting in federal elections, campaign financing, and expenditures, and the appointment of a Presidential commission to study the decline in voter participation. The Committee has also issued substantive studies through sponsorship of symposia and national conferences, and publication of educational monographs and conference proceedings. Conferences typically are intensive meetings drawing together national experts to study such issues as campaign finance, the Electoral College, the presidential selection process, the vice presidency, the use of technology in campaigns, the Voting Rights Act, redistricting, voter participation, and the Federal Election Commission.

The election process has the potential to be an extremely political issue. But, due to the fact that the Committee has scrupulously maintained a nonpolitical stance on the issues in which it has become involved, it is one of only a few groups in the country to which the Federal Election Commission, congressional committees, and state election law experts have turned for assistance in examining the soundness of electoral laws and policies and developing recommendations for change. The Standing Committee remains committed to ensuring that the nation's election laws are legally sound and are drafted to permit the broadest, least restrictive access by Americans to the ballot box.

The Standing Committee on Election Law is currently chaired by Pauline A. Schneider, a partner in the law firm of Hunton & Williams in Washington, D.C.